Preface

Over the past 12 years I have written a number of books and articles. Most, not all, have focused on questions and dilemmas regarding national security. On occasion, I have stepped outside my comfort zone, addressing additional issues. Often, I draw on my professional experiences largely based on my 19-year career in the Israel Defense Forces.

This book has been a profoundly different experience. Unlike previous writing efforts, this book has become deeply personal, forcing me to examine—in an intimate manner—the impact the Holocaust has had on my family and me. That was not my intention when I began considering this book.

The book was prompted by a question regarding the Holocaust, which led to many discussions. It was humbling to discover how little I knew about the Holocaust, much less of my family.

While reading a great deal of Holocaust-related literature, I constantly had to remind myself that I am not a historian and that my primary focus is examining the bystander from a legal perspective. That required identifying a "link" whereby the question of bystander obligation would be relevant to contemporary society. Unfortunately, innumerable examples abound. Those are discussed in the pages ahead.

Writing this book has taken far longer than previous works; there were—as any author will attest—significant ups and downs. The tone and tenor of the book underwent innumerable changes. Perhaps that is intrinsic to a book that seeks to combine the personal with the professional.

I have made an honest effort to share with the reader my family's Holocaust experiences. That, for me, became in the course of writing the book extremely important. I wanted to bring what they experienced to life. It was, obviously, not easy. My research trips to Europe were difficult;

my week-long visit to Hungary where my family suffered horribly was *brutal*.

In posing the question whether the bystander should be complicit for nonintervention, my focus was the vulnerable victim. The perpetrators of the Holocaust were not my primary interest. I leave that to the others.

What fascinates me is the bystander's decision not to intervene.

Fascinated may be an understatement; obsession may be a more accurate word. Whether obsessions are positive or negative is a matter of dispute; in this case, I would like to think of them as positive.

I could, literally, write a book about the writing of this book.

Over the past four years I have met and communicated with an innumerable number of people. Writing this book has taken me to Holland, Germany, and Hungary; I have interviewed people in the United States, Canada, and Israel. I have imposed on people's valuable time—undoubtedly, sometimes overstaying my welcome.

People willing to open their doors to a total stranger and share painful stories is remarkable to experience. Many of the conversations that made this book possible were difficult and emotional. Feelings were raw.

For me, it was essential to honestly convey their experiences and stories without doing so in an exaggerated or maudlin manner. That would be disrespectful. My sole purpose in meeting with people was to better understand the question of the bystander.

The number of roads traveled while writing this book are many—intellectually, emotionally, and physically. To travel that many roads requires the support, encouragement, patience, and understanding of friends, family, and colleagues.

All faults with this book are, obviously, mine. I have been overwhelmed by the generosity, patience, and graciousness of many, many people. The list of names is as long as the book itself.

To that end, I have chosen—after much reflection—to do a collective thank-you to many and an individualized thank-you to a smaller group. It is my fervent hope this decision will be met with understanding by those not named.

I owe an unimaginable thank-you to John Devins, Maura Fowler, Christine Hashimoto, John C. Lentz, Jr., and Jonathan Malysiak. Each made critical contributions, too numerous to count. I will be forever grateful and in their debt, safe to assume—knowing them as I do—more than they will ever realize.

Travel was made possible thanks to generous support from the University of Utah, its S.J. Quinney College of Law, and a private donor.

I leave to the reader to judge whether bystander complicity must be understood to be a crime. I truly believe it is. Regardless of the reader's conclusion, my hope is that the pages ahead will enhance understanding of the consequences of bystander inaction for the vulnerable victim.

That, for me, is the essence of the Holocaust.

"You go after what your conscience tells you to do.
Others may not agree with you on everything, but that's
irrelevant.
I think a mission can be such, even when not recognized
or accepted by others.
You follow the call of your soul."
—*Holocaust Survivor*

Introduction

"Who is to blame?" is the question at the root cause of decades-long pain.

I was the last person to swim with my cousin Dani.

I was 5; he was 14.

I told him he can't swim in the deep end (he had slight cerebral palsy.)

My mom said she made me get out of the water and told my dad to watch Dani; my dad was reading.

It is an open question if he heard her/responded to her.

This has never been discussed in my family.

When the time came to leave the pool, we looked for Dani; his twin brother, David, and I looked everywhere.

Dani was found on the bottom of the pool.

I recall like yesterday the race to the hospital.

My dad drove behind the ambulance.

How did they notify Dani's father?

There were very few phones in Israel in 1962. . . .

There was a public service announcement on the one radio station asking my uncle to call my parents.

He did. This is how he learned Dani died.

The last picture of Dani alive was taken on Friday afternoon, the day before he died.

In the picture? Dani and I.

My uncle carried it with him, in his shirt pocket, every day of his life; it is framed on my desk, at home, and in my office.

My uncle died 50 years to the day that Dani died. Saturday to Saturday.

In October 2015—within four days of each other—Dani's brother, David, and my father, Shonny, passed away.

After all these years I still wonder: "Am I to blame?"

1

My cousin Dani and I, the day before he died; he was 14, I was 5.

Running with M

I am a runner of modest achievement. I run in the wee hours of the morning. Nonrunners would call it the middle of the night. Over the years, I have participated in one marathon and a number of half marathons. I pride myself on dedication, determination, and the ability to grind.

Like thousands of other runners, I have self-imposed goals and am terribly disappointed when I fail to meet those goals. Fellow runners understand this dedication, bordering on obsession.

The act of running incorporates endless motion, occasional pain, and single-minded focus. It also provides an extraordinary time to think, reflect, and ponder. Some run alone, some run with a partner, others run in groups. I run either alone or with a partner.

With a partner, the pain seems less painful, the effort less daunting, and the opportunity to engage in conversation unique and welcome. The fresh air, the predawn quiet, and mutual encouragement allow for a rare kind of openness.

When I shared with a wonderful running partner (I will call her M) that I was the only child of two Holocaust survivors, our runs became, for me, extraordinary opportunities to explore this subject.

We had many long and probing conversations. In many ways, those conversations were the beginnings of this book. I had too few answers for many thoughtful, insightful, painful questions.

Once, I shared with M an excerpt from an essay my mother wrote shortly after the death of her mother. After that, our runs seemed to take on added meaning and depth.

M—the mother of two small children—instinctively identified with my grandmother. She fully understood the rational, clear thinking under the most horrific circumstances.

My grandmother's profound maternal instincts struck a chord. M, in awe of my grandmother's remarkable composure when facing death, focused on her bravery and the actions, or *inactions*, of others.

She asked: "How the hell did this happen?"

At its core, that is *the* question when examining the Holocaust: How did 6,000,000 European Jews find their deaths in gas chambers, death squads, death marches, and beatings? The actions of governments and regimes have been studied and written about at great length, but M's focus was not on political leaders but rather on broader society, a society made up of individuals.

The inactions, regardless of motivation, of institutions were never our focal point; we only discussed the individual who chose not to act. Focusing on the individual forced me to better understand—or at least confront—the question of the individual bystander.

This process individualized the dilemma for me. Rather than examining governments and the Catholic Church, I focused on individual responsibility and accountability. I am not interested in how nation-states acted and their rationalizations, motivations, and actions.

Although national leaders articulated and implemented policies that resulted in the murder of my grandparents, they are not germane to this book. Frankly, they did not interest me. The same is true for individual perpetrators: those who actually forced my grandparents onto the train that took them to Auschwitz or those who sealed the doors of the gas chamber behind them ensuring their deaths.

People's actions—or inactions—did not take place in a vacuum.

Studying the Holocaust required reading widely on broad themes, historical trends, and events during the years of the Third Reich. This was essential to understanding the individual actor. Of particular interest were Germany, Holland, and Hungary.

The reading, research, and interviewing had one specific purpose: to better understand the bystander. That is not to suggest sympathy for the bystander. Rather, to accurately portray and discuss the bystander, it is essential to understand conditions and circumstances. Doing so would facilitate answering the three questions below:

- How did neighbor turn on neighbor?
- How was so much suffering allowed by so many?
- To whom does society owe a duty if not to its most vulnerable?

Duty to Act

This book is about duty. It is not a history book.

Readers interested in historical analysis of the Holocaust and the Third Reich have unlimited material from which to choose.

I debated with others how much history to include; M was particularly incisive: "You can't discuss the bystander in the Holocaust without discussing the Holocaust. But there is no need to provide a history of the Holocaust. That is not what this book is." She is correct.

There are distinct voices in this book. There is the *personal voice* when discussing my family; there is the *objective voice* recounting particular events in the Holocaust; finally, there is the *persuasive voice*, hoping to convince the reader that my proposal is warranted and implementable.

Some sections are particularly conversational when I am seeking to talk with the reader. The historical summary is necessary to understand the legal argument. It is also necessary in an effort to convince the reader that history offers convincing proof that reliance on moral codes of responsibility is misbegotten.

I hope to convince the reader of the legitimacy and necessity of imposing on the bystander a legal duty to act when another individual is in harm's way. That is the primary lesson I have learned from the terrible price my family paid. It is my answer to M's question.

I define the "bystander" as an individual who observes another in clear distress but is not the direct cause of the harm. A "culpable bystander" is one who has the ability to mitigate the harm but chooses not to and must be held legally accountable for that inaction. The duty to act on behalf of the vulnerable victim I propose is a legal, not moral, obligation.

A third individual, the perpetrator, responsible for victim distress, is not essential to the duty discussion. The criminal law has sufficient provisions to address the perpetrator; law enforcement, prosecutors, defense attorneys, and judges have readily identified and articulated roles regarding the perpetrator.

The system regarding perpetrator responsibility and accountability is time tested; whether effective, efficient, and just are important points for consideration and discussion. They are, however, beyond our purview.

My sole motivation is imposing a *legal* duty—an obligation—on the bystander. I am not asking "whether"; the question is "how."

The answer is simpler than one imagines. Modern technology greatly facilitates implementation of the proposed legal obligation. The suggested requirement is less burdensome and onerous than perhaps imagined.

There is no demand for the bystander to actually physically intervene on behalf of the victim; calling for professional assistance meets the burden.

Failure to intervene on behalf of the victim is the essence of complicity. We join society because we seek security and protection. That is the core of the social contract between the individual and the state. The state protects the individual; in exchange, the individual willingly relinquishes certain liberties and freedoms. It is a quid pro quo.

However, what I am suggesting is that the duty-owed paradigm be extended beyond the state-individual relationship to the individual-individual relationship. That is particularly important when state organs are at their weakest and victim vulnerability is at its highest.

Nuance is essential to a full discussion regarding the bystander; different circumstances and conditions must be taken into consideration when articulating and implementing a duty to act paradigm.

Creating, or allowing, a wide range of exceptions to an agreed-upon rule facilitates unwarranted "wiggle room" that, ultimately, provides justification for a lack of intervention and involvement. The line is thin between acting and rationalization for not acting, between complicity and noninvolvement.

Good Samaritan Laws

Some U.S. states have Good Samaritan laws intended to minimize bystander liability if the intervention caused harm to the victim. The law, in essence, provides immunity for "doing the right thing" if rescue efforts had negative consequences. It seeks to protect the bystander whose efforts were, ultimately, harmful.

The law protects the well-intentioned bystander who does not owe a preexisting duty to the victim but, nevertheless, chose to do the right thing. The law makes sense. It is, however, no longer relevant, given my proposal.

If the bystander calls for professional assistance in a timely manner, providing appropriate officials with correct information regarding location, situation at hand, and assistance needed, then the duty-owed requirement is met. Immunity would no longer be necessary.

However, should the bystander choose not to seek assistance or not to bring the situation to the immediate attention of relevant officials, then a crime has been committed. The crime is failure to intervene, making the bystander complicit in ensuing harm that befalls the victim.

The test is binary and basic: Did you call or not?

If the bystander chose to act as demanded by the proposed law, then immunity provided by Good Samaritan laws would be superfluous. Conversely, failure to act would result in criminal prosecution—subject to prosecutorial discretion—devoid of protection afforded by Good Samaritan laws. Therefore, in the event the bystander acted in accordance with the recommended legislation, there is no need for immunity as obligations imposed by law have been met.

Impact of Runs

The many miles and the innumerable thoughtful, sometimes painful, exchanges brought into sharp focus the terrible combination of evil and passivity. Studying the Holocaust shines a harsh light on neighbors who turned on neighbors, acquaintances who did not offer assistance to acquaintances, and passersby who scurried on their way.

I read widely and broadly in an effort to better understand how such evil could be perpetrated. The willing collaboration of the Hungarians, the institutionalized accommodation of the Dutch, and the fervor and enthusiasm with which Germans responded to Hitler all shouted out to me from the books I read.

Little did I fully appreciate to what extent I would be impacted by our runs.

They enhanced my understanding of the Holocaust, taught me a great deal about my parents, and inspired me to develop a legal model that would punish those who failed to protect the vulnerable. Writing this book required examining and coming to terms with dark moments in my parents' lives.

While writing this book I asked my mother why they chose not to share their Holocaust experiences with me. Her answer was succinct: We wanted to spare you.

I am in awe of how they survived. It defies description.

Of my mother, probably the toughest, most resilient person I know, my children say: "If Hitler couldn't kill her, no one can." There is great truth in that phrase. My father's survival of a death march owes much to luck, circumstances, and good fortune. There is no other rational explanation.

M's questions were critical to my gaining a much better understanding of my parents' struggles in the face of evil. They forced me to reflect on the profound questions: How did this happen? How can I make others consider the liability of those who stood by?

Legal Argument versus Moral Responsibility

Bystander complicity was essential to the "Final Solution." I have come to view the bystander, who fails to act, as complicit in harm that befalls the victim. This is what compels me to create a workable *legal* requirement whereby duty can be imposed on the bystander. The moral obligation model is, for me, tenuous and soft. Relying on the oft-repeated phrase that "people will do the right thing" is appealing and compelling.

It makes us feel good; we feel safe "knowing" someone will come to our assistance, someone will call the police, and someone will give us haven. After all, we would certainly do the same were we to see another in distress.

Certainly, that is our expectation of ourselves, for we are moral and act in accordance with our standards of morality. That is what we have been taught; those are the articulated ground rules of contemporary society. It sounds so simple, sounds so comfortably reassuring for there is something self-congratulatory about this approach; if we do good, others will, similarly, do good.

There is a powerful disconnect between the aspirational and reality. Although we would like to believe people will do the right thing, history suggests otherwise. The hope is not cost free. Quite the opposite. Unjustified reliance is an unnecessarily risky proposition. As was discussed at great length, during those early morning training runs, historical analysis offers convincing proof that hope is unrealistic and unwarranted. There is no justification in "hoping."

Whether based on a lack of empathy or sympathy for the vulnerable individual is an open question. Clear are the consequences: enhanced victim harm. The unwillingness of the bystander to intervene greatly emboldens the perpetrator. The term "complicity" was not randomly chosen; it reflects the essence of the bystander. More than that: Bystander complicity significantly contributes to victim vulnerability.

If the consequences of nonintervention are actual injury, then the consequences of inaction must also be actual. Failure to intervene must be made a crime, prosecutable and punishable with the full force of the law. This is controversial because the bystander is not the initiator of the crime. However, failure to implement this recommendation fails victims of bystander complicity. It also ensures our individual and collective acquiescence in the face of violence and racism.

There is, of course, risk in legislating an individual be obligated to act when another is vulnerable. Readers of previous drafts and participants in various forums where I have discussed the book have made that risk clear to me. It was obvious to me such a proposal would be heavily criticized and easily dismissed.

The primary concern is that imposition of a positive obligation to act on behalf of another suggests excessive government control and a distressing lack of clarity regarding standards and criteria by which duty is to be imposed. That is a legitimate concern. The question is how to create, and implement, a workable bystander intervention model. That will come in the pages ahead.

The additional, oft-voiced concern, is that the proposed recommendation creates a culture whereby reporting to the police is the operative byword; reporting rather than providing *actual* assistance to the vulnerable. There is a dilemma: Does the bystander physically help the victim or call for help? Does the bystander call for help or report that others are not helping? These questions have been continuously posed to me.

They reflect, I believe, understandable discomfort—if not uncertainty—regarding the essence of bystander *legal* obligation. The heart of the proposal is imposition to act. The actual degrees and manner of "acting" will be discussed in the chapters ahead.

The more we discussed, the more I understood both the calamity my parents were subjected to and the obvious need to suggest a mechanism whereby future perpetrators will not benefit from bystander complicity.

For me, that is the lasting impression of our runs: the direct—as compared to indirect—contribution of the bystander to the deaths of my family members. The questions M posed forced me to this conclusion.

The personal journey, which this book has become, has two distinct elements: examining my parents' Holocaust experiences and proposing a model whereby bystander complicity does not go unpunished. By focusing on the first, I hope to convince the reader of the viability and justification of the second.

The journey has not been easy. Reading about the Holocaust, watching Holocaust-related film clips and documentaries, interviewing Holocaust survivors, traveling to Europe, and focusing intensely on the events of 75 years ago has become, for lack of a better term, an obsession.

This journey—this book—is, for me, a life project. It is intense, all encompassing, and painful. There is no happy story, with one exception:

My parents, somehow, survived. Or, as my mother says, they "won," as she defines herself as a Holocaust victor rather than survivor.

While writing this book, as the refugee crisis was exploding, my mother called me. Our conversation was short and to the point.

She was overcome with emotion watching Hungary turn its back on people in dire straits; she was outraged watching history repeat itself.

— 1 —

Where I Come From—Who I Am

My Bystander Experiences

In the course of my lifetime, I have been faced with the dilemma of whether to involve myself when others are in need of assistance. I have made right and wrong decisions; the former are not worthy of discussion, the latter weigh heavily on my conscience.

The question of whether to act or not to act is visceral to me. As a five-year-old child playing in a pool, I recognized my cousin might be in danger. I did not sufficiently speak up. My cousin drowned. This tragedy haunts me to this day. I have over the subsequent decades internalized the consequences of observing but not acting. Yes, I was only a five-year-old child. Nevertheless, the overwhelming magnitude of the event is more powerful than any rational analysis regarding the limits of what a small child can do.

That afternoon has significantly shaped my understanding of accountability, responsibility, and consequences. Obviously that event and growing up in the shadow of the Holocaust shaped my personality. The two are intertwined; separately and together they are critical to my conception of the bystander.

When faced with the decision whether to intervene on behalf of a vulnerable victim, I have not always chosen the correct path. Once I chose not to assist a homeless adult who was the subject of ugly, physical bullying by a college student.

My inaction was inexcusable. I stood but two feet from the incident and could have either prevented it or minimized harm to the homeless man. On a second occasion, at a restaurant, an individual at the next table was engaged in an anti-Semitic diatribe. I chose to ignore it.

My inaction in both instances has taught me much. Perhaps I chose the safe course out of a natural instinct for self-protection, to avoid harm and injury. If so, are we then obligated to reexamine this instinct? Is it always justified? Can there be a legal basis for liability in certain instances of inaction?

These are questions with repercussions for society. The reasons for an instinctual "no" are obvious; more compelling are the reasons for answering "yes."

According to my proposed legal definition of bystander obligation, my failure to intervene when the college student bullied the innocent homeless individual in my presence would be deemed a crime, subject to police investigation and prosecutorial discretion. The college student clearly committed a crime for he assaulted another; my crime, in the legal architecture I propose, was one of omission. I clearly had the capability to act. I chose not to.

That would not be the case regarding my conduct when my cousin drowned; actor age, capability, and situation recognition must be taken into consideration.

What about the anti-Semitism at the restaurant? Ugly, yes, but because it did not morph into incitement, the speech was protected. A crime did not occur.

Should I have said something?

What is an ethical course of action in this particular instance? Individual moral and ethical considerations are of the utmost importance, yet they are distinct from the bystander's legal obligation.

These three incidents—a drowning, unwarranted violence, and anti-Semitic speech—reflect the spectrum of daily human interaction and conduct. They are neither special nor unique; tragedy occurs in other families, random violence is a reality, and offensive speech is not unusual.

The three are distinct from the Holocaust; however, they reflect daily events and interactions in a manner the Holocaust does not. For that reason they are important: The proposed legal model regarding bystander liability must be relevant, and applicable, to daily circumstances.

Some would say fear justifies noninvolvement. However, in my experiences, fear was not the reason for my noninvolvement. I was not fearful of the college student.

Rather, I simply chose to scurry on my way, not wanting to be late to the University of Michigan football game whose kick-off was quickly approaching. Though clearly a mundane example, this gets at the essence of the bystander dilemma: When confronted with an opportunity to intervene on behalf of another, what will be the decision? To answer this question we have to examine the interaction and relationship among perpetrators, victims, and bystanders.

A Child of Survivors

My father, who had a distinguished academic career at the University of Michigan Medical School, at Haifa University, and at Emek Yizrael College (Israel) had an unfortunate fall in April 2011. His cognitive skills greatly suffered thereafter.

Conversation with him was very limited. However, for a few days in June 2015—literally "out of the blue"—we were able to discuss this book. It made for an extraordinary moment: If not for this book, we would not have had these conversations.

As discussed in the pages ahead, my father very much disagreed with my thesis regarding bystander liability. I find this perspective fascinating: It suggests an "understanding" of those who were bystanders to his Death March.

I have come to learn that, in the main, bystanders to Death Marches can be divided into four categories: those who observed but did not intervene, those who taunted and baited the Jews, those who turned violent and killed Jews, and those who offered assistance.

Unlike my father, I do not find it possible, existentially, morally, or practically, to "understand" and thereby absolve of guilt. We will return to this theme.

In 2002, I accompanied my father on what is referred to as a Holocaust roots trip. We traced the Hungary of my mother and my father, a world that no longer exists. The four-day trip was powerful, painful, and unforgettable.

Upon our return to Israel I contacted Yad Vashem, the World Holocaust Remembrance Center. I wanted a professional historian to videotape my parents for the purpose of recording an oral history. I felt it important for my three children.

I informed my parents they would be contacted to arrange the taping. My father was direct in his response: "Don't you ever do that to me again."

I felt my father's response was a lost opportunity, but respected his refusal. However, for my children's sake I felt it essential my parents record their experiences. To that end, in November 2005, my parents allowed a close friend to record their memories.

To this day, I have not been able to watch the tape.

My Mother

My mother, Susie (nee Zsuzsanna Neuser) was born in Szombathely, Hungary; her parents were Pal (Paul) and Aranka (Fellner). My grandfather worked in a bank and as an insurance salesman before becoming a partner in a sport shop; my grandmother did not work.

My grandfather came from a family of significant means; my grandmother came from a poor, religious family that moved to Hungary from Transylvania (later Romania).

My mother was an only child; my grandparents' first child, a daughter, Agi, died three months before my mother was born. My mother was raised in middle-class assimilated Budapest; she went to the ballet, enjoyed ice skating and the pleasures and benefits associated with comfortable, not wealthy, Central Europe of the 1930s.

Although my mother was not raised in a religious home, my grandmother maintained a kosher kitchen in deference to her mother. In direct

My mother, four years old.

contrast to my father, my mother's upbringing included secular activities and norms, though she attended a Jewish high school in Budapest, The Gymnasium.

My mother immigrated to Israel in 1949;[1] she and my father married in 1955. I had a wonderful relationship with my maternal grandfather; I was his only grandchild, he was my only grandfather. Even though language was somewhat of a hindrance, the bond was strong, enabling us to easily overcome barriers.

During my Bar Mitzvah training, I decided to make my maternal grandparents' last name—Neuser—my middle name;[2] my purpose was to honor them and my relationship with them. I knew nothing of their

---

1. The correct term is "made aliyah" ("act of going up"; making immigration to the Land of Israel).
2. My parents did not give me a middle name.

Holocaust experiences; this book project has enabled me to see my maternal grandparents, for the first time, as Holocaust survivors. Although I always perceived my parents as survivors, I viewed my maternal grandparents in a different light.

That is, frankly, perplexing; I have known for years my mother and grandmother hid together in Budapest and had some vague notion my grandfather was sent to a labor camp in the Ukraine.

Nevertheless, I was unable to connect my maternal grandparents to the Holocaust; perhaps the generational gulf was too wide. It was difficult enough to grasp my parents were survivors and my father's family had been murdered in Auschwitz. In any event, I failed—viscerally and emotionally—to link my mother's parents to the Holocaust. This is in direct contrast to my understanding, even as a child, of my paternal grandparents' fate.

When M asked *the* question, my initial reaction focused on my murdered paternal grandparents, Salamon and Teresa Goldberg, rather than my maternal grandparents.

As I have come to more closely scrutinize and understand the Holocaust experiences of my maternal grandparents, it is clear they were inches away from a similar fate. This has raised endless questions regarding what separates survivor from victim. One caveat: Although I accept my mother's definition of survivor as "victor," that is not, under any circumstances, intended to label the victim as "loser."

Not in the least.

My Maternal Grandmother, Aranka Neuser

Shortly after my grandmother's death (February 1980), my mother wrote the following:

On March 19, 1944, the German occupation of Hungary began and the Jewish population of Budapest was moved into specially assigned houses in special areas of the city. My parents, as did their friends, heard rumors about Jews from all over Hungary being sent to concentration camps in Poland and Germany.

My maternal grandparents.

We did not know when our turn in Budapest would come. I was only twelve years old, still quite sheltered but aware of the situation. Like all the other Jews, I wore the yellow Star of David, and I knew what it meant to be afraid. The apartment house where we lived during that time was mostly inhabited by women and children and the elderly. Men between the ages of seventeen and sixty were in work camps. There was no school for Jewish children from March 1944 on, and we youngsters did the best we could under the circumstances. We set up our own classes without teachers and we played a lot.

On October 15, 1944, the Hungarian Nazi party seized power and the relative safety of the Jews in Budapest came to an end. Four days later, at about five o'clock in the afternoon, as it was getting dark, we heard shouting below, calling us down to the courtyard. The shouts were followed by knocking on the doors, and we were told to pack a single small bag with some essentials. In the courtyard,

*men in Nazi uniforms armed with guns were beckoning us to hurry
down.*

*Mother and I went down the steps, she holding a small bag in one
hand and my hand in the other. As we reached the courtyard where
all the others were gathered, we were pushed against a wall and told
to be quiet. I was terrified; not knowing what to expect but somehow
aware that something terrible was going to happen. As we were facing
the wall my mother pulled me in front of her. I remember vividly how
I kept saying: "I don't want to die, I am too young to die and if I die I
will never see my father again."*

*I remember praying aloud "Shma Israel, Adonay Elohenu, Adonay
Echad" (Hear O Israel, The Lord our God; The Lord is One). I remember the uniformed Nazis reading the names of people in the apartment
house. I remember hearing them cocking their guns and starting to
count. I remember knowing that the end was there.*

*And I remember my mother quietly holding me in front of her,
shielding me with her body and telling me that when I heard the
guns being fired I should fall with her, under her. She told me to
wait for the dark, and only then I should try to crawl out from under
her. My mother sounded calm, holding me strong and protective
against her body, sheltering and defending her child, ready to give
her life while saving mine. Then just before they finished counting to
three, somebody with orders not to shoot appeared in the courtyard.
We were released and sent back to our apartments.*

*She faced the ultimate test of the mother bravely, willing to give her
life, and in that one supreme moment she was perfect.*[3]

Judging Others

Much has been written about the conduct of European Jewry during
the war; the phrase "sheep to slaughter" has been suggested as describing Jews going to their deaths in Auschwitz. I have heard it from many,
including Holocaust survivors with whom I have met. However, they

---

3. Susie N. Guiora, http://www.bjpa.org/Publications/details.cfm?PublicationID=17384.

have suggested the phrase does not accurately reflect what they knew at the time of their deportation. The implication is that conduct of Jews must be viewed from their perspective, rather than from a contemporary knowledge base.

At a family dinner a number of years ago, an Israeli, in his thirties, used the expression. Posed as a question, it carried enormous negative connotation. It reflects a decades-long unspoken sense in Israel that European Jews were submissive and docile in the face of danger.

This in direct contrast to the post-Holocaust Israeli self-perception as strong, self-reliant, and vigorous in self-defense. It is the image of the "weak Jew" as compared to the "strong, tanned and confident Israeli."[4]

There was palpable discomfort as all eyes turned to my father. I asked myself—during the few seconds of utter silence—how would he react? Would there be an academic discourse? Would he become deeply wounded and visibly upset? Would he give a stern look, which for me, as a child, was far worse than being yelled at?

His only comment was a terse "you can't understand, you weren't there."

There was a sigh of relief as the conversation shifted gears to other matters. Nevertheless, that moment has stuck with me. It highlights an important question: Can we judge actions of others when we "were not there"? There is something comforting about such an approach; it disinvites—discourages—judgment of a situation that defies comprehension.

As a child, I never questioned the tightly wrapped leftovers in our refrigerator. My assumption was that this is a result of my mother's Holocaust experience. Holocaust literature emphasizes Holocaust survivor's constant fear of hunger. It seemed safe and respectful not to comment; why contribute to my parents' painful memories?

---

4. Perhaps not by accident, Israeli bureaucracy is disdainful, hurtful, and dismissive of Holocaust survivors. This is an unconscionable stain on successive Israeli governments that have turned a blind eye to the plight of the remaining Holocaust survivors. On one occasion, I accompanied my mother to a Claims Office housed in the Israeli Finance Ministry; the treatment was beyond offensive and unimaginably rude. Only my clearly stated threat regarding legal action facilitated resolution of her matter.

When I was a child, emotional displays were infrequent in our house. In retrospect, perhaps, my reticence in asking questions reflected a desire to avoid conflict. Maybe that is the reality of an only child or maybe that reflects my personality. Perhaps it is the actualization of "don't judge, you weren't there"?

Without doubt, it results in many unanswered questions. Whether that is a good thing or not depends on many factors including the individual, circumstances, and a willingness to confront unpleasant, if not dark, corners in one's family history.

I chose the easy way out. For better or worse, that attitude guided me in my relationship with my parents—until the writing of this book. M's question triggered a journey with many roads.

If forced to answer her question years ago, I would have relied on stock answers reflecting hesitation to understand the Holocaust beyond a superficial level. That includes debating whether it is possible to judge, even though I was not there.

I struggled with this question. Adopting this approach is simultaneously respectful and comfortable. It also denies the opportunity to explore and truly ask complicated and painful questions.

There is also something presumptuous in assuming to know how I would act under similar, unimaginable, circumstances.

Would I have resisted being placed on a train? Would I have looked the local policeman in the eye and cursed him with every invective possible? Would I have run and trusted my physical instincts?

The correct answer is: Who the hell knows?

That is also the correct response to the bystander.

Would I have been heroic? Would I have offered food, shelter, and haven to Jews on a Death March? Would I have seen someone such as my father as a victim or as "the other"? Would I have cursed the "dirty Jew," taunted him with food, and wished him good riddance?

I would like to think not; but I do not know for sure.

What I do know is that relying on the bystanders' "positive instincts" is fool's gold. It is, at best, a lovely parable and nothing more than that. My readings, research, and interviews have had an interesting impact on me: I am more critical of the bystander than I am of the perpetrator.

The latter was "all in." Guilt clear, crime obvious, and punishment justified. For me, the perpetrator is neither interesting nor relevant to this book.

The bystander is more complicated. I have developed powerful feelings regarding the bystander. On a scale of antipathy-empathy, the bar tips in favor of the former. Not exclusively, but predominantly.

Analyzing the bystander dilemma, particularly the question of liability-complicity, requires judging. In that sense, my inherent belief of "don't judge, you weren't there" has been shaken, if not uprooted. While there is, doubtlessly, trepidation in engaging in historical judgment, it is well-nigh impossible to answer the core question otherwise.

Regarding the comment-question posed at the family dinner: I do not know if my grandparents went like "sheep to their slaughter." I think about that a great deal. Am I judging them? I am not sure. Do I wish they had resisted, fought back, told the Hungarian fascists to "go fuck themselves"?

I am not sure to what extent it would have been possible, much less effective. That is a question I leave to others.

What I do know is that answering M's question requires analyzing the inaction of the bystander. That is something I increasingly feel comfortable doing. My comfort—a terrible word given the circumstances—is predicated on the conviction that bystander intervention could have saved my grandparents.

No guarantee.

I am, however, willing to venture it would have increased their chances.

Summer 2015

In June to July 2015 I spent two weeks in Holland and Germany researching this book. I met with criminal law professors, historians, sociologists, philosophers, and commentators. The meetings served as the basis for a longer, more in-depth trip in the summer of 2016. The significance of both trips cannot be sufficiently stated. They enabled me to gain significant insight into the Holocaust bystander from a wide range of perspectives.

Furthermore, the interviews provided me with a much more nuanced understanding of historical events. The 2015 interviews and discussions can be considered as the backdrop to the 2016 discussions. Two words best describe the two trips: *journey* and *mission.* I define journey as in exploring the applicability of the theory of bystander complicity, and mission as in sharing with the reader the voices of those whom I met who spoke about those who were killed.

One word of caution: In a meeting with a Holocaust expert, whose parents hid Jews in the Netherlands, I noted that the events of 1939–1945 are my baseline regarding an examination of bystander complicity. My use of the word "baseline" was met with skepticism. I was asked to explain.

I suggested the following: The Holocaust is a terrible combination of heinous evil reflecting absolute abnormality committed by state agents and perpetrators alike. That madness was greatly facilitated by the silence of millions. However, that silence is more complicated than meets the naked eye. Not all events were what they seemed to be. That I have learned in the past few years, particularly in long meetings with Holocaust survivors, children of bystanders, and scholars.

However, there were clearly times bystanders should—and could—have acted on behalf of victims. It is in those instances the bystander failed the victim.

In the context of "baseline," if bystander complicity can be identified in an abnormal context—which the Holocaust was—then the assigning of bystander complicity in the contemporary age poses significantly less challenges.

The examples interspersed throughout this book are intended to highlight situations in a normal context when bystander nonintervention is not understandable, not excusable, and cannot be tolerated. By introducing examples from the Holocaust, imposing a legal duty to act on bystanders, in everyday dilemmas, should fall on fertile ground.

The meetings in Holland and Germany were intellectually engaging and, occasionally, emotional. The two most powerful meetings—in Maastricht, the Netherlands, and Wannsee, Germany—were of critical importance. One visit—Platform 17 in Berlin—was essential to my developing an understanding of "space" as it relates to bystander and victim. The three locations—two in Germany, one in Holland—directly confronted me *both* with the bystander and the decision-making process leading to implementation of the "Final Solution to the Jewish Problem."

Understanding the bystander-victim relationship requires recognizing the physical relationship between the two. It is what I choose to call the *"physicality"* of that relationship. That concept is germane to examining bystander liability.

Bystanders observing my father's Death March or watching my mother and grandmother scurrying from safe house to safe house were—literally—within touching distance. Victims and bystanders were in the same milieu; they occupied, physically, the same space.

They were not, however, in the same emotional space. My father, mother, and grandmother were the "other"; the sense of community and commonality shattered. Perhaps it never existed. Amos Elon brilliantly made that argument in his book, *The Pity of It All.*[5]

My father's world was exclusively Jewish; my mother's was more assimilated. However, in those critical moments both were Jewish and both were the "other." Both were within physical touching distance of people who could have provided them assistance.

Space is an essential element to understanding the symbiotic relationship between bystander and victim. Relationship is a complicated term; nevertheless, it is of essential importance to the interaction—*actual and virtual*—between bystander and victim. To be fully appreciated, shared space must be seen.

In order to maximize the learning experience I spared myself no quarter in looking evil in the eye, regardless of the emotional difficulty. I made, in the words of a friend, an honest effort to "dig in and immerse in that very painful history." I wanted, 75 years after the events, to "feel" the bystander. This is not to be confused with "sympathy" for the bystander.

In seeking to "feel" the bystander, the goal was to put myself in the bystander's shoes, to understand the physicality of his or her circumstances and to visualize events of decades ago.

---

5. Amos Elon, *The Pity of It All: A Portrait of the German-Jewish Epoch, 1743–1933*, Henry Holt and Company, New York, 2003.

Platform 17

"Platform 17" was the departure point for 50,000 Berlin Jews during the Second World War. From there, they had a final glimpse of their city before deportation to concentration camps. When standing next to the platform, the view from a nearby house was foremost on my mind. That nearby house is of paramount importance in analyzing the bystander.

"Nearby" is an understatement; a mere stone's throw is a more accurate description. Standing at the beginning of the tracks, looking at the house, in particular a window on an upper floor brought the physicality of the Holocaust into stark juxtaposition.

The phrase "beginning of the tracks" is an accurate physical description. A correct analogy is that the beginning of the tracks marked the beginning of the end for those forced onto the trains. There was no escaping that painful realization. Standing there was a solemn moment.

The house highlights the critical importance of space and proximity; it has forced me to recognize how physically close the bystander was to the victim. That physical relationship—almost touching, but not quite—is of primary importance when considering the bystander.

Platform 17, July 2015.

Saw but chose not to touch; observe but turn away. Or not turn away. Perhaps wishing the boarding Jews "good riddance."

I envisioned Jews, about to board *the* train looking up with pleading, helpless looks in their eyes; I pictured the individual in the house looking down. The "looking up-looking down" analogy is particularly powerful, capturing two distinct physical positions and two profoundly different states of mind.

What did the person from the upstairs window see when Berlin's Jews boarded the trains? What did that individual understand regarding the fate awaiting those carrying their bags and holding their children's hands? Was there *any* sympathy for a mother clutching her baby? Empathy for a father fearful for his family's fate? What was the reaction when the train door slammed shut?

How the hell did this happen?

That question was what I wondered standing at the train platform.

It is too easy to say the person at the window is the answer. Bystander complicity, as I stared at the window, is twofold: It significantly enhances perpetrator conduct and dramatically enhances victim isolation. That is the consequence of enabling.

The mental image of families with their bags watched by their fellow German citizens was powerful and disturbing. That the scene was played out in full view of the public accentuates bystander complicity.

The memorial is simple; perhaps stark is a better word. On the side of the platform are bricks conveying the following information: date, number of Jews deported that day, and deportation destination. The bareness of the memorial emphasizes the horrible emptiness and vacuum that has been left behind.

The bricks are on both sides of the platform; one stops, gazes, and moves on to the next block. According to Jewish tradition, stones are placed on graves as a sign of respect; stones have been placed on individual bricks.

The quiet is akin to a cemetery in its starkest and barest form.

Amsterdam

In Amsterdam, many of my meetings were held in a lovely corner bakery: The croissants are fresh, warm, and delicious; the cappuccino good, not great. I have eaten at this bakery many times over the years. However, it was only on this trip, when sitting at an outdoor table, did I notice two apartments across the street. The adjoined apartments are, as far as I could discern, large and comfortable.

From the apartments it is a ten-minute walk to Dam Square, twenty minutes to Amsterdam Central Station. There are other coffeehouses in this primarily residential neighborhood.

During my meetings I found myself gazing at the apartments, asking myself—hypothetically—who were the occupants in 1942 and what was their fate during the German occupation? Needless to say, the additional question was whether Jews lived in one apartment and did their Gentile neighbors provide them assistance?

I tried to visualize the deportation. I made myself focus on the fears of one family, the possible actions of the other family. This took on special meaning for me. Simply put: *When the Jewish family was deported, what did the neighbor know, do, and think?*

In the context of the bystander-victim relationship, the *visualization* of Jews walking to the train station, standing on the train platform, being forced onto the train, and having the train door slammed, not to be opened until the train arrived at a location where certain death awaited, was overwhelming and all-encompassing.

Maastricht

At the recommendation of Dutch colleagues, I contacted Professor Fred Grunfeld; rarely has a suggestion proven more beneficial and important. Professor Grunfeld's contribution to this book was enormous. It was, frankly, unintended and unplanned. When I met with him for the first time—as described below—there was no intention on my part to return to Maastricht in the summer of 2016. However, that return visit was necessary based on the initial visit.

I arrived by train to a town I literally knew nothing about. I wrote the following shortly after my visit:

Fred picked me up in his car, drove me to his house and parked the car. So far, nothing special.

As I start walking towards the house (trying to get out of the awful heat) he says, "I have something to show you, come see." (I am thinking: "dude, I'm dying of heat, let's go inside.")

The stumbling stone

He shows me a stumbling stone.[6]
And with this begins the story.
When we go inside he tells me the tale of the woman whose name is on the stumbling stone, Marcelle Antoinette Devries.

Marcelle who was born February 1906 lived in the house until August 25, 1942 when she was ordered by the SS to report to the local school. She did so in daylight carrying her bags in full view of her neighbors/fellow citizens.

The 300 Jews of Masstricht were deported in three waves (August 1942; November 1942; Spring 1943).

Marcelle was at the school for a few hours before walking at night-time a few hundred meters to the train station from which she was deported to Auschwitz.

She was gassed upon arrival, August 31, 1942.

---

6. Stolpersteine Gelsenkirchen, http://www.stolpersteine-gelsenkirchen.de/stumbling_stones_demnig.htm.

Her sister escaped/hid in Belgium, her brother escaped to Switzer-
land and her parents also survived. Fred is in contact with the brother's
son who has visited the house.

After Marcelle was deported, German soldiers lived in the house
until November 1944 when US soldiers who freed France, Belgium
and southern Holland in the aftermath of the Normandy Invasion
came to live in the house. Fred found—under the carpet—a US army
manual from 1944.

The house—five stories tall (huge)—is a national monument.

All of Marcelle's neighbors were Gentile; according to Fred, they
were the classic bystanders.

There was a street in Maastricht where 50 Jews lived. In August
1942 a bus accompanied by German SS or Dutch Police came to the
street and forcibly ordered the screaming/crying/resisting Jews onto the
bus. Watching the scene from her house was a little girl who today lives
in Maastricht.

The little girl was not a bystander; however, her parents and other
Gentile neighbors who saw and/or heard the deep anguish of the Jews
were bystanders.

Could they have acted?

Did they have the ability to either save some or all of the 50 Jews who
lived on that street?

Should they have undertaken efforts to save other Jews?

What are reasonable expectations under such circumstances?

The same questions are pertinent to those who observed Marcelle leaving her house, carrying her belongings, walking in the direction of the
train station.

In the course of my visit, Fred invited me to tour the house.

From different vantage points I could clearly imagine the "visual" of
Marcelle walking and neighbors watching. Their thoughts are, obviously,
unknown to me; their actions suggest a failure to act.

Could they have acted?

Should they have acted?

What risks would they have assumed?

Are they liable-complicit in Marcelle's death?

The hypothetical Jewish tenant in Amsterdam living across the street from the corner bakery was at profound risk for reasons whose origins were not in Amsterdam.

Obviously the deportation process did not occur in a vacuum, hence my visit to Wannsee. It would be impossible to examine the former without understanding the latter. The outcome of the Wannsee Conference held on January 20, 1942, under the leadership of SS-Obergruppenfuhrer Reinhard Heydrich, was the brutal realization and implementation of Nazi racial policy.

Wannsee Conference

On July 8, 2015, I spent two and a half hours at the Wannsee Conference House.

At the Wannsee Conference, according to Heydrich,[7]

> the Fuhrer[8] had now given his sanction to the evacuation of the Jews to the East as a further "solution possibility". . . they (the evacuees) were to be organized into huge labor columns. In the course of this labor utilization a majority would undoubtedly "fall away through natural decline.". . . The survivors of this "natural selection" process—representing the tenacious hard core of Jewry—would have to be "treated accordingly.". . . Heydrich did not elaborate on the phrase "treated accordingly.". . . Practically . . . the implementation of the "final solution" would proceed from west to east.[9]

The visit brought into clarity evil and complicity: the former because of the consequences of what was casually decided; the latter because of the extraordinary pictures displayed on the walls of the villa.

---

7. Reinhardt Heydrich, who chaired the Wannsee Conference, was one of the main architects of the Nazi regime and of the Final Solution; Heydrich died June 4, 1942, after being shot on May 27, 1942, by a British-trained team of Slovak and Czech soldiers.

8. Hitler did not attend the conference.

9. Raul Hilberg, *The Destruction of the European Jews*, Quadrangle Books, Chicago, 1961, pp. 264–265.

Friends and family had warned me about the overwhelming dissonance between the beauty and elegance of the villa and its surrounding area with what was decided there. My preparation included reading Mark Rossman's outstanding book, *The Villa, The Lake, The Meeting: Wannsee and The Final Solution*.[10] Nevertheless, I was caught totally off guard when entering the majestic gardens, much less the beautiful house.

This is what I wrote before the visit:

Well, today's trip is to the essence of the essence *as I have afternoon meetings at Wannsee; friends and family who have previously visited the villa universally commented on the absolute stunning beauty of the place.*

Have been told by others that one of the things that makes the visit so overwhelming, in addition to what the fellas discussed oh so casually while eating well, followed by cognac and cigars (at his trial, Eichmann noted Heydrich invited him for three glasses of cognac) is the extraordinary elegance of the backdrop and the stunning civility of the neighborhood.

BTW: I fully intend to have a cigar at end of the day (call it my victory cigar).

Seventy-three years after Heydrich and fourteen other senior German officials met for two hours to discuss—and decide—the "Final Solution of the Jewish People," I stood in the rooms where the fate of my grandparents was sealed, overcome with nausea.[11]

While they were deported from Nyíregyháza and murdered in Auschwitz, it was at *that* villa that their days were officially numbered.

The Social Contract

Duty to act is the essence of the social contract even if the victim has been defined as the "enemy" or "the other."

---

10. Mark Roseman, *The Villa, The Lake, The Meeting: Wannsee and the Final Solution*, Penguin Press, London, 2002. http://www.amazon.com/Villa-Lake-Meeting-Wannsee-Solution/ dp/0141003952/ref=sr_1_1?ie=UTF8&qid=1436336488&sr=8-1&keywords=Mark+Roseman+T he+Villa+The+Lake+The+Meeting.
11. It is recommended to view this documentary, https://www.youtube.com/watch?v= URSNN5mnI2g.

Decisions must be made quickly. Consequences of inaction are, oftentimes, inevitable. Preventing harm requires real-time intervention. Failure to intervene on behalf of the other led to the deportation of my grandparents to Auschwitz, the beating of others, and the forced march of my father.

Although they had been defined as the enemy and as the other, they were victims. No more, no less. The bystander owed them duty. Failure to intervene is complicity; it is a violation of the social contract.

Could that deportation have been prevented? Could someone have saved my grandparents as they made their way to the train station in May 1944? My father believes the answer is "no" because Hungarians (meaning non-Jew) did not have the "obligation to intervene because the Jews were not human beings."[12]

In writing this book I interacted with many people in Europe, Israel, and the United States. In response to an earlier draft, I received the following thoughtful response:

(p)rotection of the vulnerable is one of the essential elements of the social compact.

I would maintain it is not THE essential element. I'm sure no Talmudic scholar, for sure, and I would suspect many moral authorities (though not the Third Reich or ISIS) recognize the primary moral imperative of self-preservation and preservation of family with relatively less responsibility for those less directly related (clan, friends, fellow citizens wherever that concept came from, etc).

You mention self-preservation earlier in your intro. Self-preservation sometimes conflicts with the moral responsibility to protect the vulnerable.

I would consider the essential issue as how to define when protection of the vulnerable trumps these other fundamental moral values. And then to define legally when the obligation of the bystander to protect the vulnerable overrides the moral and legal right of self-preservation.[13]

The reader and I disagree whether protection of the vulnerable is *the* essence of the social contract. Our disagreement is not mere semantics.

---

12. Conversation May 28, 2015.
13. Private correspondence; email in my records. At sender's request, identity is anonymous.

The difference between "degrees" of essence is of critical importance regarding bystander obligation.

From the perspective of the victim, bystander obligation is of the essence. It can be the difference between life and death; if duty is fungible, the perpetrator is emboldened and, largely, unhampered. A social contract without clear contours, reflecting mutability, would minimize victim protection.

The duty-to-intervene obligation reflects societal recognition that victim distress must be concretely and definitively addressed. There can be no middle ground with respect to duty; either it is, or is not, imposed. While the duty proposed is not cost free, the consequences of bystander inaction far outweigh costs associated—directly or indirectly—with the proposed duty.

The Bystander

Clarity and precise articulation described my father's verbal abilities. I do not recall asking him to clarify what he said, whether in Hebrew or English. He spoke a number of other languages, but I speak only those two. His writing skills were equally impressive.

He avoided verbiage and pretentiousness in his verbal exchanges. Answers to questions were well considered, thoughtful, articulate, and concise. You asked a question, you got an answer.

When we conducted the conversations, his intellectual capacity was significantly hampered. Of that, I have no doubt. However, his answers, which I have included verbatim, were mirror images of my father at his best. Clear, articulate, and devoid of unnecessary words. Bullshit was not in his DNA.

My father disagrees with my thesis that intervention obligation be imposed on the bystander. My mother joined him in voicing skepticism. When I asked why, they had a similar response: The Jew was the enemy and the bystander's primary obligation was self-protection.

I asked my father whether he considered requesting assistance from villagers observing the Death March. They saw him. He saw them. There was clear eye contact. There was almost physical contact. The distance separating them from him was no more than arm's length. He did not feel they would harm him. The question was whether they would help him.

With respect to that he was clear: "From their (villagers') perspective we were just Jews not worthy of their care or attention."[14] In response to my follow-up question *if* you would have asked for help, he was similarly clear: "I wouldn't have asked for help and wouldn't have received any help as it was not acceptable that Jews would ask for help."[15]

Our conversation focused on bystander duty and the relationship between Jews and Gentiles in Hungary. It was important for him to emphasize Jews were not a part of Hungarian society:

> *They were Jews* but *(his emphasis) not Hungarians; the Jews were Jews and the Hungarian bystander did not have* any *(his emphasis) identification with Jews. There were two populations: Jewish and non-Jewish, and intervention would endanger the non-Jew.*
>
> *The non-Jew certainly wouldn't endanger himself for the Jew, even if he knew him previously.* Jews were simply different and non-Jews had no obligation to save them. *(his emphasis)*

I am unable to fathom the depths of despair of European Jewry on the eve of its destruction. I can but try to understand the sense of utter hopelessness my father expressed regarding villagers witnessing his Death March.

He had no expectation of, or from, them. His isolation and despair was of no interest to them. He did not feel they would harm him. But he certainly did not think they would help him. He harbors no anger toward them.

I have replayed our conversations numerous times in my mind. He did not agree that I videotape or record. I believe he was concerned how he looked and sounded. I tried to convince him otherwise to no avail. I typed as he spoke.

---

14. Conversation May 28, 2015.
15. Ibid.

The twin notions of hopelessness and isolation have stuck with me. He was very clear regarding both. For him, the witnessing villager had no reason or intention to offer him assistance. It is, I believe, for that reason my father disagreed with my recommendation. For him, there cannot be any expectation of, or demand from, the bystander in the Holocaust.

However, the fact the state defined the Jew as the enemy does not—and must not—excuse the bystander. That is too easy an explanation for bystander nonintervention. That is too convenient a rationalization for a neighbor turning a back on a neighbor or the callousness expressed in a complaint filed (1941) by a nearby resident of Mauthausen:

> In the Concentration Camp Mauthausen at the work site in Vienna Ditch, inmates are being shot repeatedly; those badly struck live for some time, and so remain lying next to the dead for hours and even half a day long. My property lies upon an elevation next to the Vienna Ditch, and one is often an unwilling witness to such outrages. I am anyway sickly and such a sight makes such a demand on my nerves that in the long run I cannot bear this. I request that it be arranged that such inhuman deeds be discontinued, or else be done where one does not see it.[16]

In other words, a bystander sees, yet chooses to ignore. That is the essence of the bystander.

Gordon Horwitz compellingly explains this in describing Mauthausen inmates forced to build a camp in Redl-Zipf for Germany's V-2 rocket testing:

> The futile inmate search for townspeople, or for an acknowledgement of their own presence, added to their sense of isolation. The townspeople sensed the existence of the inmates nearby in the darkness but denied their reality.[17]

---

16. Gordon J. Horwitz, *In the Shadow of Death: Living Outside the Gates of Mauthausen*, The Free Press, New York, 1990, p. 35.
17. Ibid., p. 89.

Bystander Categories

I propose creating three distinct bystander-victim scenarios:

1. Anonymous Bystander-Faceless Victim
2. Neighbors
3. Desensitized Bystander-Disenfranchised Victim

The first theme will be examined through the lens of Death Marches (October 1944–May 1945), the second theme will be examined through the lens of the deportation of Dutch Jewry, and the third theme will be examined through the lens of the deportation of Hungarian Jewry.

To facilitate understanding of the relationships, I propose the following delineation: In the Death Marches, the victims were "faceless" and the bystander "anonymous," reflecting the lack of a preexisting relationship between the two categories.[18] Regarding Holland, the definition that best describes the bystander-victim relationship is "betrayal by neighbors";[19] in the Hungarian paradigm the relationship is defined as "desensitized bystander" and "disenfranchised victim."

To determine legal culpability of the bystander, it is necessary to distinguish *bystander* conduct and knowledge, from *perpetrator* intent and conduct and *victim* knowledge and conduct. The three principal actors— perpetrator, bystander, and victim—must be examined from three distinct perspectives: conduct, knowledge, and capability. Determination of culpability is dependent on that three-part analysis impacted by conditions and circumstances.

It has been suggested the bystander's primary obligation to self and family outweighs duty and responsibility to the other. In addition, the decision oftentimes quickly made to scurry on, thereby ignoring needs

---

18. Death March survivors have noted that the conduct of bystanders ranged from offering assistance to "taunting" with food to participating in the killing.

19. I had initially intended to define the relationship as "neighbor," but conversation with a Dutch Holocaust survivor shed important light on the concept of "betrayal." The theme of "neighbor" is based on the important book by Jan T. Gross, *Neighbors: The Destruction of the Jewish Community in Jedwabne, Poland*, Penguin Books, New York, 2001.

of others, has been repeatedly offered as reflecting the reality of human interaction.

More correctly it reflects human "noninteraction."

Nuance is essential to a full discussion regarding the bystander. Doubtlessly, sensitivity to different circumstances and conditions must be taken into consideration when articulating and implementing a duty to act paradigm.

However, creating, or allowing, a wide range of exceptions to an agreed-upon rule facilitates "wiggle room" that, ultimately, provides justification for a lack of intervention and involvement.

The line is thin between acting and rationalization for not acting, between complicity and noninvolvement. Whether to provide assistance or turn a blind eye was doubtlessly impacted by an assessment predicated on self-interest and self-preservation.

Although an understandable human trait, one of the critical questions this book addresses is whether that instinct legally justifies inaction. To understand the relationship between bystander and perpetrator is no less important than examining the relationship between bystander and victim.

The relationship between perpetrator and victim, in the context of the Holocaust, can be neatly summarized as hunter and hunted.

Complicity is at the core of our undertaking.

— 2 —

My Family

With two exceptions—my senior honors thesis at Kenyon College on the Warsaw Ghetto Uprising and a keynote address at an Anne Frank Conference—the Holocaust has never been a source of academic inquiry, or priority, for me.

Rather, it has been a largely undiscussed, looming dark cloud hovering over me for decades. The adage that second-generation Holocaust survivors—referring to children of survivors—live in the shadow of the Holocaust applies to me. There are times I think the adage was articulated with me in mind.

I am consistently struck by broad gaps in my knowledge regarding events leading up to the Holocaust, and of the Holocaust itself. On some level I always wondered—but not much more than that—about the Death March my father survived.

However, other than knowing that the march was from the Bor Labor Camp (Yugoslavia) located 200 kilometers southeast from Belgrade where he was a prisoner in forced labor conditions to Hungary, I had no information. I was, evidentially, satisfied with that minimal information.

My Father in Bor

I never researched Bor, never looked at pictures, and barely knew where it was. For me, it was sufficient to know he had been in a work camp, was freed, and made his way to Palestine. The details were not particularly important to me.

I knew that in the aftermath of the German occupation of Hungary, he was taken from Budapest to Bor that summer. During our Holocaust roots trip (2002), we visited the bus depot from which he was transported to Bor in June 1944. He went willingly; announcements were posted in Budapest, informing Jews where to report.

During our visit, I asked him why he reported; his answer was succinct: "Because we were ordered." I do not know the fate of Jews who disregarded such call-ups. Similarly, I do not know if my father suspected the hardships that awaited him or whether he questioned his survival skills and abilities.

As far as I know, he was not previously acquainted with those who accompanied him to Bor. If so, he did not mention anyone, with one exception brought to my attention in subsequent years. There are, however, doubts whether this person was, indeed, sent to Bor.

My father did not share with me—nor did I ask—what route the bus took to Bor; I do not know if he knows. My focus was not on transportation logistics; sufficient for me was that he survived.

While researching this book, I found pictures of Bor in books and online. I eagerly looked at the pictures, wondering whether I could identify my father.

My initial reaction, when viewing the pictures, was a sense of being overwhelmed.

I tried to visualize him there, working, trying to stay alive, fighting the cold, and wondering: "Will I survive?" Pictures depict a bleak, hard, and harsh place. Jews and others worked in copper mines essential for Nazi war efforts.[1] For that reason, the camp was of significant strategic importance, particularly in the later stages of World War II.

To me, Bor looks like an awful place where no good could occur. Prisoners were tortured to death in Bor. I have read horrific accounts of the camp commander tying Jews to trees and whipping them to death. This was news to me; for some reason, I was under the impression prisoners were not killed in Bor—died from labor-related causes, yes; murdered by their guards, no.[2]

---

1. https://bhiweb.files.wordpress.com/2011/12/summary2011-11-09.pdf.
2. Whether justice was meted out to perpetrators in postwar tribunals and judicial proceedings has never been a point of interest to me. I never researched, much less read, transcripts of the Nuremburg trials. Only recently have I inquired what fate awaited the commander of the Bor

This distinction was important for my father. On the few occasions we discussed Bor, he was careful to add that killing did not occur. Whether he did not know this or chose to "hide" it from me is unclear to me.

I do not know what my father's particular task was, nor do I have any insight into his daily life. I do not know where he slept, what he ate, with whom he lived, or his thoughts regarding survival. My assumption is that his world was focused on survival. It is hard for me to imagine that his daily motivation and energies extended beyond that.

He spent five months there. My father never shared with me details of the work he performed. According to Richard Frucht, Bor was "one of the most brutal German extermination camps":[3]

> *The Hungarian Jewish labor battalions, especially the ones deployed on the eastern front or at mines in Bor, Serbia, as well as the Romanian labor battalions doing road and railway construction work and the Bulgarian labor battalions that were used for the expansion of the infrastructure, some of them also working for the OT, had to suffer from horrendous living and internment conditions similar to those in the concentrations camps of the SS.*[4]

In his book about his time in Auschwitz, *If This Is a Man*, Primo Levi[5] shone a powerful light on the daily reality of imprisonment in the Holocaust.

Primo Levi brilliantly captured the essence of loneliness, the unknown, and fear. I have come to associate those adjectives with the starkness depicted in pictures of Bor. However, I am unable to conjure mental images of my father in a place where the camp commander personally tortured people to death.

---

labor camp, Lieutenant Colonel Marányi. That was only in response to my mother asking me while I was writing this book.

3. Richard C. Frucht, *Eastern Europe: An Introduction to the People, Lands and Culture*, Volume I, ABC Clio, Santa Barbara, CA, 2005, p. 393.

4. http://www.jewishvirtuallibrary.org/jsource/judaica/ejud_0002_0007_0_06611.html (last viewed November 22, 2015).

5. Primo Levi, *If This Is a Man*, Abacus, London, 1987.

Perhaps my father did not know this. Where he slept, where he worked, if he was beaten, if he was humiliated, and with whom did he confide and share his fears and dreams are questions forever buried.

Primo Levi's poignant descriptions of interactions with other prisoners have been helpful in trying to answer my unanswerable questions. Levi's austere, yet vivid account gives insight into my father's five-month period of imprisonment. I assume he was consumed with thoughts regarding the fate of his parents and brother; I assume survival was the uppermost thought and priority. I assume he wondered how to get home without knowing what, if anything, there was to return to and how to avoid being killed in a godforsaken place in Yugoslavia.

Primo Levi writes:

We fought with all our strength to prevent the arrival of winter. We clung to all the warm hours, at every dusk we tried to keep the sun in the sky for a little longer, but it was all in vain. . . . today it is winter. We know what it means because we were here last winter; and the others will soon learn. It means that in the course of these months, from October to April, seven out of ten of us will die. Whoever does not die will suffer minute by minute, all day, every day: from the morning before the dawn until the distribution of the evening soup we will have to keep our muscles continuously tensed, dance from foot to foot, beat our arms under our shoulders against the cold.[6]

My father's present was in the hands of a murderous regime whose primary focus was the killing of Jews at the expense of its quickly failing war effort. He did not know his parents had been deported to Auschwitz, much less that they were murdered. He was also unaware his brother survived the Holocaust until they met in Hungary[7] and understood their family was no more.

---

6. Ibid., p. 129.
7. I do not know where in Hungary.

My father's liberation document.

Yugoslavian partisan fighters, under the command of Josip Broz Tito, freed my father. After his escape, he made his way to Bulgaria where he received forged documents enabling him to travel to Palestine through Turkey and Lebanon.

My father arrived in Palestine in November 1944.

Holocaust Survivors

Conversations with Holocaust survivors are a challenging paradox: Their experiences are beyond painful and their suffering is beyond the realm of the understandable, for the horror of the Holocaust is unimaginable. Yet, their experiences are tragically real and recalled with painful detail. To interview a Holocaust survivor requires stepping into a world that once existed and seeking to understand the essence of survival and horror.

The conversation is stark in its candor and painfully honest and brutal in its horror. Soft-shoeing is not acceptable.

In June 2014 I spent a week in the Netherlands meeting with Holocaust survivors, scholars who have researched the Holocaust in specific and genocides in general, and members of the Dutch media. My first interview on a rainy, dreary Monday morning was with an academic who is a Holocaust survivor.

Because of a slight misunderstanding, we did not meet where we had intended. As a result, he was a few minutes late. He had agreed to meet with me based on the recommendation of someone he knew whom I had never met.

To my surprise he chose not to sit opposite me at the coffee house but rather next to me; it quickly became clear why. After a quick—*very quick*—exchange of pleasantries, he looked at me directly and spoke clearly: "I will only talk with you if you tell me why you are writing this book. Do not bullshit me."

It was a directive, not intended as a polite request nor taken as such. The physicality of the encounter was powerful: A distinguished academic sat down next to me, and he dispensed with the usual social niceties. He wanted to determine my intentions. His manner sent a clear message.

Slightly taken aback, I looked him square in the eye and replied: "This is the only way I know to honor my father and his experiences."

With tears in his eyes, he said: "I know you are telling the truth. Let's get to work." The conversation taught me a great deal about the Holocaust in Holland. It also highlighted the complexity of this undertaking.

In the course of writing previous books and articles, I have interviewed hundreds of people from an extraordinarily wide range of disciplines, perspectives, personalities, agendas, and locations. None of these, however, prepared me for writing this book. My emotional investment in the subject matter was inescapable and constant.

I was, truly, engaged in an effort to come to grips with how the Holocaust directly impacted my parents and by extension, me. Interviews and research increasingly took on a double significance—understanding the bystander in the Holocaust and understanding my parents in the Holocaust. The two, on some level, have merged. This initial interview clearly confronted me with this reality.

For that, I am deeply grateful to this most distinguished, direct, and powerful academic.

My Father's Family

In the late 1930s, Hungarian Jewry, like much of European Jewry, was confronted with pressing questions regarding its future. To what extent that reality was internalized on a wide scale is an open question to this day.

German Jewry seemingly had greater insight into Hitler's true intentions than other Jewish communities. The number of German Jews who fled in the mid-1930s is telling. Kristallnacht was a powerful indicator of the regime's hatred and violence directed at German Jewry. Nevertheless, warning signs were, as we tragically know today, clearly missed.

My father, age 2.

My paternal grandmother and uncle.

My father, whose given name is Sandor Goldberg,[8] was born June 25, 1925. He was his parent's second son; my uncle, La'yosh, was four years older.

My father grew up in Nyíregyháza, in northeastern Hungary. In 1941 the town's population was 59,156 of which 4,993 (8.4 percent) were Jewish;[9] Hungary's population was 9,340,000[10] of which 825,000 were Jewish, less than 6 percent of the entire population.[11]

---

8. My father and uncle changed their name from Goldberg upon arriving in Palestine/Israel; while my father chose to spell the name Guiora, my uncle spelled it Giora. With respect to why they changed their name, see http://forward.com/news/309070/for-israelis-hebrew-names-are-about-autonomy-not-assimilation/ (last viewed October 26, 2015).

9. http://www.jewishgen.org/Yizkor/pinkas_hungary/hun379.html.

10. http://www.populstat.info/Europe/hungaryc.htm.

11. http://www.ushmm.org/wlc/en/article.php?ModuleId=10005457.

My paternal great-grandfather.

In 1949, Nyíregyháza's population was 56,334;[12] its Jewish population in 1946 was 1,210.[13] In 1946, Hungary's population was 9,040,000[14] of which 200,000 were Jewish.[15]

The dominant member of my father's Orthodox family was his maternal grandfather, a much-revered rabbi, and the final authority on all family-related matters.

My grandfather—Salamon Goldberg—a schoolteacher, deferred to his exalted father-in-law on all decisions, with one exception.

And that exception is central both to this discussion and to why I am alive.

---

12. http://nepesseg.com/szabolcs-szatmar-bereg/nyiregyhaza.
13. http://www.jewishgen.org/Yizkor/pinkas_hungary/hun379.html.
14. http://www.populstat.info/Europe/hungaryc.htm.
15. http://www.ajcarchives.org/AJC_DATA/Files/1946_1947_13_Statistics.pdf.

In 1939, my grandfather, an ardent Zionist, believed that leaving Hungary and moving to Palestine (as pre-state Israel was called) was essential both to save his family and to participate in the building of the Jewish homeland. My great-grandfather rejected that notion; akin to countless other rabbis throughout Europe who believed moving to Palestine/Israel before the return of the Messiah was theologically inconceivable.

Any such thought was "verboten"—absolutely and totally, consequences be damned.

In other words, until the Messiah arises, Jews must not—cannot is more accurate terminology—live in the Promised Land. While my grandfather had attained the documentation required for leaving Hungary and traveling to Palestine, his father-in-law rejected the idea. As a result my father's family stayed in Hungary. The decision had overwhelmingly tragic consequences. The same is true for countless other Jewish families.

All members of my father's family, with the exception of my father, uncle, great-grandfather, Rabbi Yaacov Gottleib, and great-grandmother, Regina Gottleib, were deported in the summer of 1944 to Auschwitz where they were murdered. Why?

My great-grandparents passed away of natural causes before the deportations began; my father and uncle were saved because my grandfather sent his sons to study at the Ferenc József Országos Rabbiképzö Intézet[16] in Budapest. While both had traumatic Holocaust experiences, neither was deported to Auschwitz.

My grandfather's decision to send his sons to a non-Orthodox high school in Budapest saved their lives; it also, undoubtedly, earned him the eternal wrath of his father-in-law. I am not privy to the details of the conversation in which my great-grandfather issued his "edict." My understanding is the tone was harsh, decisive, and absolute.

My great-grandfather, Rabbi Yaacov Gottleib, was wedded to his orthodoxy in the fullest and strictest sense of the word.

My grandfather, Salamon Goldberg, acted in accordance with parental instinct and a desire to create a better life for his children. It was based on the Zionist ideal of living in the Jewish Homeland.

---

16. Franz Joseph National Rabbinical Seminary.

The story cannot be sufficiently appreciated without recognizing that the world of eastern Hungary, for its Orthodox Jewish population, was largely marked by onerous poverty, strict discipline, deep religiosity, and isolation from Gentiles. It was, in many ways, a "closed world" marked by minimal interaction with outsiders. My father's world revolved around family, cheder (religious school), and religion.

It was a rigid world with little knowledge beyond its own self-enclosed borders; its values and ethics were deeply grounded in Jewish law and tradition, largely separated from its Hungarian neighbors and their ways. While Nyíregyháza was not a small village akin to the shtetls[17] of Jewish Poland and Russia, its Orthodox Jewish population had a shtetl mentality regarding the world beyond its walls.

The below describes Jewish life in Nyíregyháza in the aftermath of the German occupation:

When the Germans came to Nyíregyháza on April 11, 1944, they prepared a list of the local Jews, then prepared a local ghetto using the streets whose majority were local Jews. On April 14 the transportation to the ghetto began of village Jews in the district. They were forced to go by foot, and only the very old and babies were taken in wagons. Those who became weak on the way were hit by gendarmes, and many fell before they reached the ghetto. On the way they were robbed of their valuables.

. . . The density in the ghetto was difficult. About 11,000 were crowded together into 123 houses. The food situation was especially bad, for those who were expelled into the ghetto from nearby villages, more than half of those in the ghetto, were not permitted to bring any food with them. The Jewish Council was very helpful.

. . . On May 5 the inhabitants of the ghetto were transported, some to Nyíregyházairjes, others to Harangod, and the rest to Sima. These three places were in desolate areas, and so the Jews of the Nyíregyháza area, were cut off from communication with them.

17. http://www.myjewishlearning.com/history/Modern_History/1700-1914/traditional-jewish-life/Shtetls.shtml.

The expulsion from the ghetto was done in a very humiliating way. The expelled people were transported through the city square, and a loudspeaker played marches.

In their new places they lay on the ground without a roof.

An epidemic of White-spot typhus began to spread, and many lost their lives. In addition to this, the gendarmes tortured these people cruelly in order to extract confessions from them about hidden valuables and money. Some of the Jews, including the leader of the Orthodox community, died of torture, and others committed suicide because of their great suffering. When at last the transports to extermination camps began, many of the people in the camp looked at it as near-salvation from their tortures.

On May 12 the Jews of Nyíregyháza began their journey to Auschwitz from the railway station of Nyíregyháza where they walked eight kilometers through pouring rain. Under the blows of the gendarmes, the local non-Jewish population stood and looked at the sight without reaction. The transports continued until the end of the month.[18]

To understand the temerity of my grandfather's decision requires recognizing the absolute power of the Rabbi father-in-law. Tragically, my father has but a handful of family pictures from his childhood. The one picture of my great-grandfather suggests a severe, yet attractive, man, with a clear sense of self and purpose regarding his position and status.

The image of Moses on Mount Sinai often ran through my mind when I saw the picture as a child. His obstinacy, absolute belief in God's ways, and failure to consider alternative viewpoints led to the death of his family. Actually, it directly resulted in their murder.

According to a family relative,[19] my grandmother's final words, as she stood in the selection line at Auschwitz, were "Who'll take care of the boys?"

That painful question spoken by my grandmother when she understood that death was but minutes away represents the "perfect" confluence

---

18. http://www.jewishgen.org/Yizkor/pinkas_hungary/hun379.html.
19. The circumstances of her survival are not known to me.

between the evil of the perpetrator, the indifference of the bystander, and the helplessness of the victim.

What my grandparents understood regarding the intentions of the Third Reich is unclear and will never be known. Although rumors were rampant, in retrospect often accurate, proof of the destruction of European Jewry was not readily available to its intended victims.

That, however, does not inherently excuse the nonaction of the bystander. After all, the legal paradigm I am proposing examines bystander culpability independently of the victim's knowledge and action.

When my grandmother—standing in the women's selection line, separated from my grandfather who was either in the men's selection line awaiting death or had already been murdered—uttered her words, she bore no responsibility for the fate that awaited her.

My grandmother's father issued the decree that, ultimately, proved to be her death sentence. My great-grandfather—the exalted rabbi—ordered his daughter and son-in-law to not leave Hungary for Palestine.

However, the inaction of the Hungarian bystander must be viewed *separately* from my great-grandfather's ruling and my grandparents' obedient fulfillment of it.

Victims

To understand the Holocaust is to delve into a world marked by relentless anti-Semitism and unparalleled state-sanctioned violence, all enabled by collaborators and bystanders.

Determining bystander liability requires assessing *knowledge* regarding victim vulnerability and potential harm. What did the bystander know? What did the bystander see? What was the bystander's understanding of the situation?

Similarly, *victim knowledge* of immediate and future dangers must be examined. Did the victim understand and recognize the threat posed by the perpetrator? However, victim ignorance does not free the bystander of liability.

Bystander knowledge must be examined separately from victim knowledge. Whether Holocaust victims understood their fate does not necessarily mean bystanders recognized potential harm. The opposite is similarly true.

Were my great-grandfather less guided by religious dogma, perhaps he would have been more cognizant of various warning signs regarding what the future held. It was 1939 when my grandfather ignored his father-in-law.

I do not know what, if anything, they knew of Hitler, Kristallnacht, or concentration camps. The family did not own a radio. My father once shared with me the excitement of hearing on a neighbor's radio news that a Hungarian Jew won a major sporting event.

The point of the story was not the championship, but rather how he heard the news—from someone else's radio. For me, this highlighted the closed world in which my father was raised. I never asked him when was the first time he heard of Hitler.

I write these lines while reading *Mein Kampf.* I am sure my great-grandfather never heard of Hitler's book; whether he would have understood Hitler's intentions and evil is a question with no answer. What is clear is that absolute conviction prevented him from listening to younger voices seeking a drastically different future than the world he fervently believed in.

Although my great-grandfather was tradition bound, deeply wedded to an unforgiving orthodoxy that did not brook dissent, he was, ultimately, a victim, albeit spared the gas chamber. To view him otherwise is to misconstrue the essence of the victim. Not viewing him as a victim creates unjustified and unwarranted "wiggle room" for those directly and indirectly responsible for the Holocaust.

His unwavering belief and profound conviction directly contributed to a terrible tragedy. Dogmatism facilitated the cruel fate that awaited family members who dutifully obeyed Rabbi Gottlieb's directive. However, that does not—under any circumstances—make his family anything other than victims. Too many "ifs" are required to enable a seismic shift in a centuries-old worldview based on tradition, rigidity, and profound faith.

My great-grandfather, like countless others, made a terrible mistake in judgment that doomed his family to death. Nevertheless, that decision does not change the status of my great-grandfather or grandparents: All were *victims* of Nazi perpetrators *and* Hungarian bystanders.

They were victims of the deportation and murder of 450,000 Hungarian Jews in a remarkably short period of time. To ascribe guilt to my great-grandfather for his decree, or to my grandparents for not defying him, is to misunderstand the true meaning of victim and culpability. It is also to free perpetrators and bystanders of guilt for their role in implementation of the Final Solution.

Perpetrators fully intending to implement the Final Solution bear responsibility for the deaths of millions. However, bystander complicity enabled the unremitting efforts of the perpetrator.

Without bystanders, perpetrators would not have been able to commit the worst crime in human history. Although bystanders were neither initiators nor instigators, their nonintervention was essential to the perpetrators.

The following quote describes those watching my grandparents make their way to the train station in Nyíregyháza:

> *Tens of thousands visited the board fence of the ghetto to peer inside or voiced content at seeing crowds herded towards the train station; at the same time tens of thousands most likely pitied the Jews' plight. But millions simply lived their lives, went to work, and tried to get by under the deteriorating conditions of war. They paid no attention to the tragedy unfolding around them.*[20]

---

20. Zoltan Vagi, Laszlo Csosz, and Gabor Kadar, *The Holocaust in Hungary: Evolution of a Genocide*, AltaMira Press, Lanham, MD, 2013, p. 279.

— 3 —

Historical Background

Introduction

To understand the Holocaust requires studying German history, the history of anti-Semitism in Europe, and the history of German Jewry. The Holocaust was the manifestation of Hitler's Final Solution. Destruction of European Jewry was a—perhaps *the*—goal of the Nazi regime. Hitler's obsessive focus on destroying European Jewry required reallocating and diverting critically needed resources from the actual war effort.

European anti-Semitism has been a reality for centuries; nevertheless, the Holocaust represents something profoundly different. The very term, *Final Solution*, reflects an unmitigated desire to eradicate European Jewry. The Nazi regime created a killing machine intended to defeat the Allies and, simultaneously, implement the Final Solution.

Hitler and others developed the twin goals, remarkable in their scope, ambition and efforts, over the course of years. However, it was, ultimately, Hitler's combination of rhetoric, power, and vision that led to the Holocaust and enabled its extraordinary results and impact.

The aftermath of Germany's defeat in the First World War, the signing of the Treaty of Versailles, and Germany's economic condition directly contributed to Hitler's rise to power. Hitler brilliantly manipulated the treaty's impact—direct and indirect—on the German economy and psyche.

The consequences of Germany's defeat in the First World War and the terms of the Treaty of Versailles were dramatic and ultimately tragic. Military defeat was debilitating. In addition, the impact of reparations imposed on Germany by the treaty dramatically reinforced the sense of crisis and strengthened the need to assign blame for defeat and its consequences.

The deep social and economic crisis greatly facilitated the rise to power of the National Socialist party. The crisis, seemingly, could be resolved with a strong government predicated on nationalism, antidemocratic principles, and racism.

The rise of the National Socialists reflects Hitler's ability to capture the national mood of anger, despair, and resentment. Hitler's genius was to focus those powerful sentiments on the German Volk's common enemy: Jews and Bolsheviks. The "Jewish International Conspiracy," in conjunction with the Bolsheviks, was, according to National Socialist ideology, the cause of Germany's travails following World War I.

The deliberate targeting of German Jewry reflected Hitler's obsessive anti-Semitism; while its roots are a matter of historical controversy and debate, the consequences are not. The deliberate decision, as reflected in a series of legislative decrees, culminating in the Nuremberg Laws, was to remove Jews from German society. In other words, National Socialist ideology intended to delegitimize German Jewry by targeting Jews as "the enemy."

Jews as Enemies

"Jew as enemy" is essential to understanding the Holocaust. The combustible confluence of economic plight, national anger, and relentless hate-filled rhetoric tragically occurred when Hitler ascended to power. However, as historians have consistently and correctly noted, Hitler rose to power through democratic means, not by revolution or force.

The National Socialist party represented the will of the German people. To what extent is a matter of historical debate. What is not subject to debate is the fact that the party did not "grab power" illegally or violently.

While the regime targeted non-Jews, primarily intellectuals, gypsies, suspected communists, and dissenters, the primary focus was Germany's Jewish population. The irony, akin to other Western European countries, was that the Jewish population viewed itself as culturally assimilated. German Jews believed their cultural, scientific, and educational contributions to Germany including active and, in some cases, decorated participation in World War I protected them from Hitler's threatening words and their possible, dire, consequences.

There were certainly those who recognized the fate that awaited them, but the overwhelming majority of European Jewry was at the mercy of the Nazis and their collaborators throughout Europe. For a variety of reasons, the manner in which Western European Jews were killed significantly differed from how the majority of Eastern European Jews were killed. The former were largely deported to concentration camps, whereas the latter were largely bludgeoned and shot to death near their homes.

The deportations that occurred throughout Western Europe did not occur in Eastern Europe; the brutal murders throughout Eastern Europe largely did not mark Nazi conduct in Western Europe. Nevertheless, their ultimate fate was similar—death. In Eastern and Western Europe alike, the active participation of the bystander was essential. The same holds true for Central Europe, including Hungary.

Delegitimization of German Jewry had distinct aspects to it; the economic exclusion of Jews and confiscation of their property was of particular importance. Professor Raul Hilberg noted the connection between economic expropriation and the subsequent annihilation of Jews.

German Jews were seen as "the enemy"; delegitimization, if not dehumanization, of the Jews was a mainstay of National Socialist ideology. Blaming "the other"—primarily Germany's Jewish population—was a dominant motif of the political, social, and economic landscape in the aftermath of Germany's defeat in World War I. An integral aspect of this was "the regime's expropriation of the Jews, a vast campaign of plunder with few parallels in modern history."[1]

Formal disenfranchisement of Jews was essential to implementation of the new racial order at the core of Nazi ideology. Jews comprised 1 percent

---

1. Richard J. Evans, *The Third Reich in Power*, Penguin Books, New York, 1978, p. 378.

of Germany's pre–World War II population; nevertheless, the regime was defined by its obsession with, and unabated hatred of, its Jewish population.

The consistent dehumanization of Jews created the environment whereby the Holocaust could occur. The Nazi regime's relentless emphasis on racial policy targeting Jews, habitual criminals, the handicapped, homosexuals, and gypsies, was implemented through a variety of means including sterilization and eugenics. According to Richard Evans, there was a "comprehensive drive to remove elements the Nazi's considered undesirable, including above all the Jews, from German society."[2]

The effort and focus was to "remove Jews from German economy . . . and discourage people from patronizing such (Jewish) establishments, or to pressure local authorities into placing their orders elsewhere."[3] Implementation required that "(A) whole range of state offices was involved in driving Jews out of economic life."[4]

Jews in Germany, Holland, and Hungary

Post–World War I Germany was ripe for powerful and charismatic leadership that would restore pride, nationalism, and honor. Jews were portrayed as part of a global conspiracy and, thereby, as the enemies of German pride and nationalism. It was necessary for Hitler to convince German citizens to turn against fellow German citizens.

The betrayal of German Jews by German nationals was essential for the Third Reich's intended destruction of European Jewry. Betrayal was essential to the mass deportations of Hungarian and Dutch Jews, particularly the latter.

After all, in both Holland and Germany, Jews had—seemingly—been fully assimilated into mainstream society. While Hungarian and Dutch Gentiles betrayed their Jewish population to a foreign power, German citizens betrayed Jewish citizens to their own regime. That is distinct from collaborating with an occupier.

2. Ibid., p. 503.
3. Ibid., p. 382.
4. Ibid., p. 388.

German Jews assumed the anti-Semitism that defined Jewish-Christian relations in other European countries was distinct from their interaction with neighbors, colleagues, and associates. That same assumption largely defined Dutch Jewry. In Holland, like Germany, the extraordinary contributions of Jews to culture, medicine, politics, literature, arts, and music have been thoroughly documented.

Although anti-Semitism was a reality in both countries, the assumption, if not perception, was that Jews were accepted by mainstream society. This is in direct contrast to the historically violent anti-Semitism that defined Jewish life in Eastern Europe.

Like Germany and Holland, Central Europe reflected a perception of Jewish assimilation; however, in the end, the fate remained the same: death.

As one thoughtful observer noted in a conversation regarding implementation of the Final Solution: "In Western Europe there was sense of betrayal whereas in Eastern Europe there was no surprise."[5] That sense of betrayal was heightened because, in the words of a dinner interlocutor, "Dutch Jewry was not 'Hasidic looking'[6] and therefore looked like everyone else."[7]

The difference should not be minimized. In large part, Dutch and German Jews were secular and assimilated physically resembling their Gentile countrymen. In contrast, Hungarian, Polish, and Russian Jews were more religious; the farther east one traveled, the less assimilated they were.

Hungarian Jews, including my father's family, more closely resembled Eastern European Jews than Jews in Germany, Holland, Belgium, and France. The significance is the following: Hungarian Jews, such as my grandparents, had limited interaction with non-Jews, living a largely insular existence separated from mainstream Hungarian society. This bears particular importance in understanding the bystander-victim relationship.

---

5. Private conversation; notes in author's records.
6. The reference is to Orthodox Jews with distinctive clothing.
7. Private conversation; notes in author's records.

The Times

Needless to say, these were no ordinary times. Christopher Browning's book[8] compellingly and graphically addresses actions of ordinary men in a time that was anything but ordinary. Browning's book is not about the bystander; rather it is about ordinary men who commit terrible crimes against vulnerable and defenseless victims.

Their actions, as horrific as they may be, did not occur in a vacuum. The book highlights the combustible combination of racism, anti-Semitism, and relentless propaganda and hatred.

The racism, hatred, and anti-Semitism that motivated the ordinary men of Police Battalion 101 reflected the milieu of the bystander in Holland, Hungary, and the Death Marches. The tone and tenor of the Holocaust were undoubtedly dictated by Hitler, but Daniel Goldhagen suggests German culture and ethos are inherently anti-Semitic, driven by "dark forces."[9]

The argument is persuasive; it sheds light on the German bystander who betrayed fellow Germans. That is, while Hitler bears ultimate responsibility for the Holocaust, the killing of 6 million Jews required the perpetrator's active participation and the bystander's nonintervention. To understand post–World War I Germany requires recognizing the confluence between Nazi ideology and rhetoric and a German public that responded, in large part, positively and actively.

A word of caution is necessary: There was opposition to the regime.[10] To suggest the public was a monolith would be historically inaccurate. Brave voices did speak out. However, to exaggerate the extent and depth of domestic German opposition to the Nazi regime would, similarly, misrepresent history.

Hitler's anti-Semitism was intoxicating, hysterical, and remarkably effective. His speeches were electric, charismatic, and unsophisticated.

---

8. Christopher R. Browning, *Ordinary Men: Reserve Police Battalion 101 and the Final Solution in Poland*, Harper Perennial Modern Classics, New York, 2013.
9. Daniel Goldhagen, *Hitler's Willing Executioners: Ordinary Germans and the Holocaust*, Vintage Books, New York, 1997.
10. See Hans Fallada, *Alone in Berlin*, Penguin Books, New York, 2010; Inge Scholl, *The White Rose: Munich 1942–1943*, Wesleyan University Press, Middletown, CT, 1970.

The themes were consistent: Jews were to be blamed for Germany's defeat in the First World War, for Germany's failed experiment with democracy in the aftermath of the First World War, and for Germany's failed economy. The concepts reflected basic principles of fascism, nationalism, and racism; Hitler would return Germany to its glorious roots.

The Nazification of society required systematic synchronization of all institutions. This was in accordance with Nazi ideology demanding absolute loyalty to the Fuhrer and regime. The motif articulated primarily by Hitler, Himmler, Goering, Goebbels, and Heydrich was that Jews endangered "the very survival of Germany and of the Aryan world."[11]

The regime benefited from the passivity of the church. As Professor Friedlander writes:

> [D]uring the decisive days . . . no bishop, no church dignitary, no synod made any open declaration against the persecution of the Jews in Germany."[12]
>
> Berlin Bishop Otto Dibelius in a confidential Easter missive to provincial pastors said: "One cannot ignore that Jewry has played a leading role in all the destructive manifestations of modern civilization.[13]

According to Friedlander, the Confessing Church, of which Dietrich Bonhoeffer was a leading light, primarily expressed support for non-Aryan Christians but not to Germany's beleaguered Jewish community, even while the regime was engaged in the formal disenfranchisement of Jews. The indifference, if not outright anti-Semitism, of the church justified bystander noninvolvement.

The apathy, at best, of leading religious leaders contributed to the climate that increasingly defined the Nazi regime. Individual conduct is affected by distinct factors; the deafening silence of religious leaders facilitated the regime's efforts to remove Jews from the country's social fabric.

---

11. Saul Friedlander, *Nazi Germany and the Jews 1933–1945, Abridged Edition*, Harper Perennial, New York, 2009, p. 17.
12. Ibid., p. 17.
13. Ibid., p. 18.

The conduct of Pope Pius XII during the Second World War is a matter of historical controversy; whether the Pope was "indifferent" as some have suggested or anti-Semitic as others have argued, is beyond the scope of this book. However, "it is hard to escape the conclusion that the Pope, like so many others in positions of power and influence, could have done more to save the Jews."[14]

While an exaggeration to suggest the Catholic Church could have saved European Jewry, religious leaders could have been much more vocal and forceful in their opposition to the measures increasingly implemented by the regime.

Historical Developments

Jews comprised less than 1 percent of Germany's pre–World War II population. Their exclusion—dictated by the Nazi regime—from the country's social and economic fabric was the new reality for Jew and Gentile alike.

In the words of Herman Goering: "I would not want to be a Jew in Germany."[15]

This exclusion was largely met by passivity from the population at large. Former colleagues and neighbors benefited from the new situation. Professor Raul Hilberg refers to such individuals as beneficiaries, distinct from bystanders.[16]

It is a matter of debate among historians whether the Jewish population fully appreciated the significance regarding the change in their circumstances. Clearly, the overwhelming majority did not recognize the horrific fate that awaited them. That, however, does not excuse the complicity of the bystander.

The litany of measures below demonstrates the regime's determined march regarding German Jews. The recounting highlights the alacrity with which the Nazis implemented their racial policy. The measures

---

14. http://www.jewishvirtuallibrary.org/jsource/anti-semitism/pius.html.
15. http://www.tabletmag.com/jewish-news-and-politics/194680/kristallnacht-amos-guiora.
16. Raul Hilberg, *Perpetrators, Victims and Bystanders: The Jewish Catastrophe, 1933–1945*, Harper Perennial, New York, 1992.

clearly isolated Jews from larger German society, thereby enhancing their vulnerability.

The Gentile population's passivity contributed to the successful implementation of the measures below. The majority of Germans "acquiesced,"[17] the churches "kept their distance,"[18] and the laws ensured a "permanent framework of discrimination" replacing arbitrary terror.[19]

On March 5, 1933, the Nazis received 37 percent of the votes and obtained a majority in the Reichstag in the aftermath of a coalition formed with the German National People's Party. Shortly thereafter, the first concentration camp was established when Himmler officially inaugurated Dachau on March 20, 1933.

On April 1, 1933, a boycott of Jewish shops was ordered by the regime. The boycott failed largely because of the population's passivity that, according to Friedlander, did not "show hostility to the 'enemies of the people' party agitators had expected."[20]

The boycott was preceded by enactment of the Enabling Act that granted full legislative and executive powers to the chancellor; in its immediate wake the SA[21] forcibly closed shops and attacked and killed Jews. According to Evans, the boycott "failed to arouse popular enthusiasm";[22] nevertheless, 37,500 Jews emigrated from Germany by the end of 1933.[23]

In accordance with Hitler's statement that Jews were a "subversive, parasitical element who had to be got rid of,"[24] on April 7, 1933, the Law for the Restoration of the Professional Civil Service 2 was passed. According to Paragraph 3: "Civilian servants of non-Aryan origin are to retire . . . anyone descended from non-Aryan, particularly Jewish, parents or grandparents. It suffices if one parent or grandparents is non-Aryan."[25]

On April 11, 1933, Jewish attorneys were excluded from the bar; on April 25, 1933, the Law Against the Overcrowding of German Schools

---

17. Friedlander, p. 52.
18. Ibid., p. 53.
19. Ibid., p. 55.
20. Ibid., p. 10.
21. Stormtroopers.
22. Evans, p. 15.
23. https://www.ushmm.org/wlc/en/article.php?ModuleId=10005468.
24. Evans, p. 15.
25. Friedlander, p. 11.

and Universities was passed, which limited enrollment of new Jewish students to 1.5 percent of new applicants with the overall number of Jewish students not to exceed 5 percent.[26]

In September 1933 Jews were forbidden to own farms and to engage in agriculture, and in October 1933 Jews were barred from belonging to journalist associations and from positions of newspaper editor.

Jews were the targets of laws, regulations, and restrictions; forty Jews were murdered by stroomtroopers by the end of June 1933.[27]

On August 2, 1934, upon Hindenburg's death, the German army swore allegiance to Hitler (by name) rather than to a particular office or constitution.[28]

In September 1935 the Nuremberg Laws were announced at the annual party rally in Nuremberg. The Nuremberg Laws distinguished between citizens of the Third Reich entitled to full political and civil rights and subjects deprived of those rights.

As a result of the Nuremberg Laws, a Jew was "subjected to special legislation that marked him out as a citizen with inferior rights and provided repressive regulations governing his everyday life."[29]

The increasingly weakened economic condition of Jews, predicated on Aryanization of the German economy, led to the destruction of economic means of subsistence for Jews.

Kristallnacht

Kristallnacht must be viewed as the bitter prelude to the Holocaust. It "was the culmination of more than five years and nine months of systematic discrimination and persecution."[30]

On November 7, 1938, Herschel Grynszpan shot German diplomat Ernst vom Rath in Paris. Grynszpan's family, Polish Jews living in

26. http://www.yadvashem.org/odot_pdf/Microsoft%20Word%20-%205420.pdf.
27. Evans, p. 15.
28. http://www.historyplace.com/worldwar2/triumph/tr-fuehrer.htm.
29. Frank Bajohr, *"Aryanisation" in Hamburg: The Economic Exclusion of Jews and the Confiscation of Their Property in Nazi Germany*, Berghahn Books, 2002, p. 193.
30. http://www.tabletmag.com/jewish-news-and-politics/194680/kristallnacht-amos-guiora.

Germany, were ordered expelled by the regime and transferred to refugee camps whose conditions were dire. This was made clear to Grynszpan in a correspondence he received from his family.

Vom Rath died of his wounds on November 9; word reached Hitler shortly thereafter while attending a dinner commemorating the 1923 Beer Hall Putsch. Upon hearing the news, Hitler left the dinner. Speaking on his behalf, Goebbels, in essence, called for a program directed against Jews. Historians describe events of the next two days as "spontaneously planned."[31]

On November 9 and 10, 1938, "hundreds of thousands danced in wild frenzy while millions watched approvingly."[32] There were "eyewitnesses in every corner of the Reich"[33] as ordinary German citizens either directly participated in or passively condoned a horrific orgy of violence against Jews, their property, and their synagogues.

More than 1,000 synagogues were set on fire or destroyed. Ninety-one Jews were killed and over 30,000 Jewish men ages sixteen to sixty[34] were sent to concentration camps. There they were tormented and tortured for a number of months.

Over 1,000 of those arrested met their deaths in the camps. Rampant looting and violence in a hate-filled atmosphere in over 1,000 cities, towns, and villages in Germany and Austria characterized the two days.

According to Frank Bajohr:

> [T]he significance of the November Pogrom as a radicalising factor cannot be doubted. The pogroms that were stage-managed after the murder of Ernst vom Rath . . . marked both the highpoint and the end of "mob anti-Semitism." . . . They destroyed the basis of the economic livelihood of the Jews within a few months.[35]

Following Kristallnacht, the "First Decree on the Exclusion of Jews from German Economic Life" was enacted, banning Jews from all

---

31. Ibid.
32. Ibid.
33. Ibid.
34. Representing 25 percent of all male German Jews.
35. Bajohr, p. 224.

remaining occupations and calling for dismissal of those still employed without any compensation. This measure was intended to complete the process of Aryanization:

> [I]n the repressive climate of the "Aryanisations of 1938," it seemed clear to all of those involved in the process that the final "de-Judaisation" of the German economy was inevitable and that it was now only a question of time when it would take place.[36]

By 1939, the "remaining Jews in Germany had been completely marginalized, isolated and deprived of their main means of earning a living." In the aftermath of Kristallnacht, Hitler began discussing the physical annihilation of Jews.

It is for that reason that Kristallnacht is appropriately termed the bitter prelude to the Holocaust. Anti-Semitism, as traditionally understood, was about to be replaced by the ideology of the pogrom of November 9 to 10, 1938. This can be understood to be the beginning of the Holocaust.

Bajohr's commentary regarding the ramifications of Aryanization is particularly important regarding the bystander:

> [B]ehavior of the material beneficiaries of the process (Aryanisation) is indicative of the erosion of moral standards in the German population, and of the extent of the moral indifference with which the Germans reacted to the extermination of the Jews.[37]

---

36. Ibid., p. 196.
37. Ibid., p. 291.

— 4 —

Death Marches, Holland, and Hungary

Bystander in the Holocaust

Pictures are powerful storytellers. Pictures starkly depict people standing by, watching elderly Jews being bludgeoned to death. I have seen endless pictures of people standing by the roadside, watching columns of Jews forced to march.

I view pictures with great interest, trying to comprehend the mindset and rationale of the bystander. I am drawn to those standing by, watching while "the other" was humiliated, beaten, deported, and brutally murdered.

The Nazi regime was intent on destroying a largely helpless prey that posed, with very few exceptions, no challenge and much less resistance. Every Holocaust survivor reflects resistance and opposition. The overwhelming force, resources, and unmitigated determination Germany allocated to the Final Solution is unparalleled in quantity, quality, and single-minded purpose.

The relevant question, regarding the bystander, is what did the bystander know at the time and what reasonable measures could have been taken to minimize harm to the vulnerable. Although the focus of this book is on the bystander, that examination cannot be undertaken in a vacuum.

It is essential to understand the times and circumstances of the bystander and victim alike; while separate, their worlds intertwined, if not overlapped. Understanding one helps to explain the other. Failure to understand one imposes significant difficulties regarding understanding the other.

In order to determine the bystander's capabilities to provide assistance to the victim, we must delve into their respective worlds. To determine legal culpability of the bystander, it is necessary to distinguish *bystander* conduct and knowledge from both *perpetrator* intent and conduct and *victim* knowledge and conduct.

In the Holocaust, bystander-victim interaction—or more accurately noninteraction—occurred in extraordinary circumstances, oftentimes unimaginable in their brutality and horror.

However, limits must be imposed on the extent to which conditions and circumstances mitigate culpability. Otherwise, the impact of "duty-to-care" legislation will be rendered meaningless. The bystander faces choices—some easy, many difficult. Failing to act is also a decision; its impact may be tragic and irreversible.

In the Holocaust that suggests either coarse anti-Semitism or passivity to a degree I neither understand nor accept. Some scholars suggest bystanders need to be perceived as beneficiaries, soon to occupy apartments and property of deported Jews.[1]

The bystanders, who stood by, enabled the killing of millions. Yugoslav partisans freed my father, and an elderly Gentile woman risked life and limb to bring food to my mother and grandmother. Nevertheless, my parents' predicament reflected bystander complicity.

The positive intervention of a few does not diminish the culpability of the perpetrators or complicity of the bystanders. I find bystander "inaction" more compelling, perhaps more complex, than the "action" of the camp guard, the murderer in the street, or those responsible for arresting and deporting Jews.

The essence of the bystander is seeing harm to a vulnerable victim and yet choosing to ignore. The Holocaust reflects a total breakdown

---

1. See, in particular, Raul Hilberg, *Perpetrators, Victims, Bystanders: The Jewish Catastrophe 1933–1945*, Harper Perennial, New York, 1992.

of the social contract Rousseau, Locke, Hobbes, and others brilliantly articulated.

Exploring that cooperation, in the context of the bystander, is essential to analyzing the crime of complicity. Nuance is essential to a full discussion regarding the bystander: Different circumstances and conditions must be taken into consideration when creating a duty-to-act paradigm. There are, nevertheless, limits to tolerating nuance and understanding circumstances.

At some point, failure to act is complicity and meets the test of a crime of omission. Creating a wide range of exceptions to a rule facilitates unwarranted "wiggle room" that, ultimately, provides justification and rationalization for a lack of intervention and involvement. The line is thin between acting and offering explanations for not acting; unquestionably, the consequences to the vulnerable are profound, possibly fatal.

Analyzing the bystander requires exploring the bystander's reality, perception, and knowledge. That is not intended to excuse the bystander's conduct or offer an apology for inaction on the bystander's part; it is, however, essential to exploring the relationship between the bystander and the victim. Otherwise, the discussion is devoid of context. Understanding forces impacting bystander decision making are essential to understanding why the bystander chose not to become a rescuer. In other words, why did the bystander stay a bystander and not become an "upstander"?[2]

In a similar vein, to understand the circumstances, distress, and travails of the victim requires exploring the Death Marches, deportations, and occupation from *their* perspective. Doing so will facilitate understanding the consequences of the bystanders' decision not to intervene.

To fully engage bystander liability, it is essential to understand the conditions of those most in need of assistance and intervention. In many situations, whether on Death Marches or on the eve of deportation, Holocaust victims were literally at "death's door" with few, if any, opportunities to escape the dire straits that awaited them.

---

2. Martha Minow, *Upstanders, Whistle-Blowers, and Rescuers*, Koningsberger Lecture delivered on December 13, 2014, Utrecht University, the Netherlands.

The Death Marches

The Death Marches were, more often than not, marches to nowhere.

With Allied victory increasingly clear, and great concern on the part of concentration camp guards and commanders regarding their fate should they fall into Soviet hands, many camps were evacuated. The Death Marches occurred as the Nazi war effort was on the verge of defeat. The Third Reich would shortly surrender to Allied Forces.

However, the evacuation did not mean those held in the camps were to be released; rather, guards and prisoners alike left the camps and marched. To where is an open question.

Many marches were a continuous, endless circular march covering a wide swath of land and territory devoid of purpose or direction. In many instances, Death March commanders were soldiers, rather than officers, marching without orders or instructions.

Death March survivors recall the seeming pointlessness of the marches, expressing a sense that the marches were devoid of cohesion, plan, and destination. The brutality of the Death Marches was particularly vicious; those too frail to walk at the ordered pace were killed or beaten and abused.

Repeated testimony of Death March participants sheds light on those who stood by the wayside watching. They saw—or chose not to see— individuals marching through towns, villages, and cities in obvious distress. Those marching were helpless and hopeless.

With few exceptions, the bystander did not offer assistance or solace. In some instances, the bystander became a participant and directly harmed those marching. What makes the Death Marches particularly poignant is that World War II was nearing its end. Yet, in the overwhelming majority of marches, bystanders failed to provide assistance to individuals who posed, from an objective perspective, no threat to their well-being or safety.

A view of the Death March from Dachau passing through villages in the direction of Wolfratshausen. German civilians secretly photographed several Death Marches from the Dachau concentration camp as the prisoners moved slowly through the Bavarian towns of

Gruenwald, Wolfratshausen, and Herbertshausen. Few civilians gave aid to the prisoners on the Death Marches. Germany, April 1945. (KZ Gedenkstaette Dachau)[3]

Accounts of Death Marches suggest these were hurriedly ordered, an escape more than an organized, strategic military maneuver. These were evacuations from concentration camps.[4]

Labor camps and concentration camps were largely marked by order and discipline; marches were largely marked by disorder and lack of discipline. Both were very violent. Disconnect between the two—under the direction of the same guards—was both powerful and disorienting.

Guards and prisoners shared something powerful—a focus on survival and fear: The guards feared the Russians; the prisoners feared the guards and villagers. Both were rational.

It was widely assumed among German commanders and soldiers that Russian soldiers would be unsparing, brutal, and relentless when confronting their German counterparts. Operation Barbarossa—the June 1941 German invasion of Russia—was ruthless and unforgiving.

Fear and anxiety among German soldiers were fully justified; after all, they knew all too well what they had done while seeking to defeat Russia. Letters from German soldiers to their families make that very clear:

Tout est juste dans l'amour et la guerre.[5]

Reports of Death Marches emphasize participants' primary focus on survival. That focus required walking as ordered, not drawing the attention, if not wrath, of camp guards who led the march. Falling behind, not keeping pace with the march, all but guaranteed instant, violent death.

Exhaustion, hunger, minimal clothing with, literally, rags for shoes were no excuse. The "European cold" was a physical, emotional, and psychological reality. Pictures of Death Marches are, frankly, difficult to look at.

---

3. http://www.ushmm.org/wlc/en/media_ph.php?ModuleId=10005162&MediaId=6126.
4. http://www.ushmm.org/wlc/en/article.php?ModuleId=10005162 (last viewed November 20, 2015).
5. http://english.stackexchange.com/questions/29659/can-someone-explain-the-phrase-all-is-fair-in-love-and-war (last viewed November 20, 2015).

In writing this book I have pored over available pictures trying to "put myself in the shoes" of those marching "to nowhere." The effort is very difficult, emotionally and cognitively.

Pictures depict an unfathomable combination of fear, hunger, cold, uncertainty, and brutality. Compounding that painful visual is the bystander. A Death March forced a greatly weakened individual to contend with the physical elements and brutal guards.

Were that not enough, there was an additional factor—the villager through whose town the march passed.

The villager is the bystander.

In studying Death March pictures, I have been drawn to the villagers watching Jews march by on their streets, in their towns. On some level, they fascinate me. I have spent countless hours asking myself: What did they see? What did they think? What did they comprehend? Being on a Death March meant ignoring expressions of hate, if not worse, from local villagers and hoping—against hope—for acts of human kindness.

The testimony of Olga Albogen who survived a Death March from Neustadt to Bergen-Belsen is both painful and powerful:

A: So when the Russian front was advancing we started to march by foot in the snow—it was so cold. And we were marching and rushing—they were rushing us.

Q: They were cruel, the soldiers?
A: Very cruel. They were shot one after the other and they threw them on the side for the rest of them to see.

Q: Did it happen to you that through these marches people on the way tried to help you?
A: No, no way, no way. They didn't come near us.

Q: You did not see any people?
A: Even if we saw them—from the curtains they were peeking out and watching and looking, but nobody came near us, no. And then they said to them, to the village people, that we are criminals, you know? They didn't know that we were there for no reason at all, just

because we were Jews. They are criminals, so why should they give anything for criminals. So where was I?[6]

In the Death March paradigm there was rarely, if ever, a preexisting relationship between victim and bystander. In deportations of Dutch and Hungarian Jewry there were, if not preexisting relationships, at least preexisting acquaintances and familiarity.

The witness to Death Marches saw "faceless and nameless" individuals marching—straggling is the more appropriate word—in the harshest of winter conditions with the most meager of clothing and provisions.

Unlike the deportation process, and the word *process* is important to the discussion, the marches were leaderless, aimless, and unimaginably brutal. This description is telling and powerful:

We marched through towns where people tried to help us by throwing pieces of food toward us. Not all German civilians could feel the suffering of other human beings. In some places the residents were openly hostile to us. They laughed at us when the SS prevented us from catching the little morsels of apple or bread. They teased us and cursed us, calling us schmutzige Hunde *(filthy dogs).*[7]

What did the townspeople see?

When the march began I could not see the end of our procession. Now, after four weeks on the road, I could see the end of the column which had been getting shorter each day.

Two hundred or maybe four hundred emaciated wretches were crawling on the road. We looked hideous, our unshaven faces covered with filth, our hair breeding grounds for lice.

The stench from our unwashed bodies was indescribable. The stinking odor was overwhelming, making it almost impossible for us to breathe.[8]

---

6. http://www.yadvashem.org/odot_pdf/Microsoft%20Word%20-%203750.pdf, Yad Vashem Archives O.3-10335.
7. Joseph Freeman, *The Road to Hell: Recollections of the Nazi Death March*, Paragon House, St. Paul, MN, 1998, p. 56.
8. Ibid., p. 55.

With respect to assistance:

> *There were inhabited areas where prisoners were met with no or very few acts of kindness from the residents. This occurred during the night marches when only the occasional sympathizer would come out to meet them.*
>
> *Another reason could be that most of the inhabitants (in such cases usually German) did not feel any sympathy for the prisoners or were even openly hostile towards them. For some of the German residents of Upper Silesia who had been unable or unwilling to believe information about Nazi crimes the sight of Auschwitz prisoners passing through their village or town came as a complete shock, often expressed with exclamations such as: "This cannot be true!" or "This is beyond belief!"*[9]

Death Marches from Bor

In September to October 1944, Jews detained in Bor were divided into two groups. The first group set off toward Hungary, and the second group stayed in Bor.

I do not know what they were told, when were they told, what their individual and collective reactions were, how much time there was to prepare, and what, if any, were their provisions, food, clothing, and otherwise. I also do not know what information the guards had.

In September 1944, due to the deteriorating military situation, the Germans decided to evacuate the mines. Servicemen were ordered to move north in two waves.

The first contingent left in mid-September. On the way, Hungarian-speaking Swabian (ethnic Germans) and Bosnian SS troops treated their charges with brutal ferocity. On the night of October 7 to 8, between 700 and 1,000 men were machine-gunned into mass graves at Cservenka by the SS.

---

9. Andrzej Strzelecki, *The Evacuation, Dismantling and Liberation of KL Auschwitz*, Auschwitz-Birkenau State Museum, Oświęcim, Poland, 2001, p. 152.

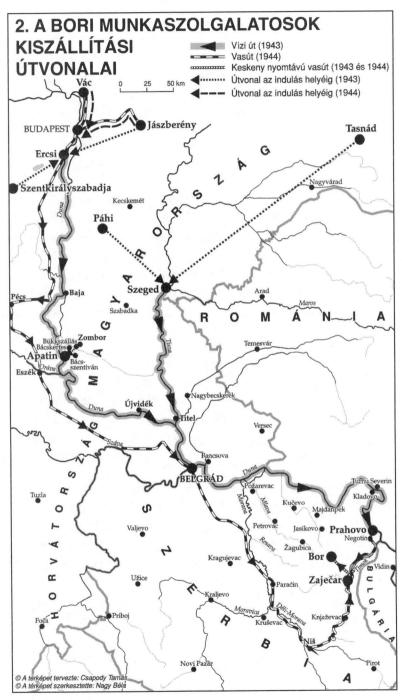

Bor and the surrounding area

Miksa Singer survived the massacre:

Ethnic German SS took over the command of our unit and they beat us up severely right away. After that they arranged us into two groups and set us off immediately. While marching away we could see the other group set off for Mohács being lined up in groups of 20 and then we heard machine guns rattling.

Later, Hungarian soldiers shot randomly into the straggling column of survivors.

Survivors of the first Bor contingent were marched on from the western border toward the interior of the collapsing Third Reich, to the camps of Dachau, Buchenwald, Sachsenhausen-Oranienburg, and Flossenbürg.

The second group that set off from Bor at the end of September fared much better. Soon after leaving, the convoy was attacked by Yugoslav partisans.

They executed the most bloodthirsty Hungarian officers and soldiers on the spot and the servicemen were set free. Some of them joined the ranks of the partisans.

Merchant Gyula Vészi was lucky enough to be in the second contingent and was liberated by the partisans:

Warrant officer Torma departed from this life five minutes later. Then we selected a few people from among the guards who had behaved decently towards us. We gave them prisoner clothes with stars and took them with us. The rest were executed by the partisans on the spot.[10]

I am unfamiliar with the basis for determining whether an individual belonged to the first or second group. Was this a hurried, panicked decision reflecting recognition of the rapid advance of the Russian Army?

My father was assigned to the second group. I do not know why. I owe my life to that fact. Similarly, details of the selection process regarding "Group One" or "Group Two" are unknown to me.

According to my father, there were rumors regarding the fate of the first group. The unknowns of my father's march far outweigh the known.

---

10. http://degob.org/index.php?showarticle=2032 (last viewed November 22, 2015).

Did my father seek to escape from the march before Tito's partisans freed him; was he beaten by guards during the march; did he believe the rumors regarding the first group and if so, did he assume death was imminent; did he draw comfort from others or was the essence of the march individual survival based on unimaginable will, determination, and resolve?

With respect to the villager, my father, as I learned in our three conversations in June 2015, had no expectation. My father believed that for the villager, he was the enemy, the actualization of the "other" to whom no help or assistance was to be offered.

In other words, my father did not believe the villager owed my father any duty. There was, according to my father, no "social contract" between villager and Death March participant; no relationship existed before the march, none existed during the march.

My father recalled "taunting" by villagers—the extending of a hand with water only to be quickly pulled back. He illustrated it by holding his arm out, hand cupped, arm withdrawn. Commensurate with the physical taunting were looks of hatred and contempt. There were no offers of assistance, words of comfort, suggestions of respite, or offers of solace.

While Tito's partisans freed my father, villager nonintervention exacerbated his predicament. Villagers understood my father and others were in distress, otherwise, why would they "taunt" with offers of assistance?

Is that not indicative of recognition that another human being is in need of help? Does the clearly weakened condition of my father and those marching with him not impose a duty on the villagers to keep their hands outstretched while holding a cup of water rather than cruelly withdraw?

If the Serbian villagers viewed the Jews as enemies, or at least as "the other"—as my father suggested—does that release them of obligation to provide assistance?

The physicality discussion presented in the context of Platform 17 is relevant to my father's paradigm. There are three distinct and separate actors—the marchers, the commanders/guards, and the villagers. It is clear guards on Death Marches were brutal. There is little doubt regarding that. However, their brutality was directed at the Jews, not the villagers; their victims were the prisoners purportedly marching—under their command—back to Hungary.

Although command, in this context, is loosely defined, the Jews were subject to the whims, violence, and hatred of their guards. The villagers, by all accounts, were not.

There are no reports of guard violence directed at the villagers; similarly, there are no reports that villagers felt threatened by the guards. Clearly, the marchers did not pose a threat to the villagers. Such a suggestion would defy logic, by any and all stretches of the imagination.

My research has found no evidence of violence directed at villagers by Jews on Death Marches. The relationship between Jews and villagers can best be described as the former in desperate need of assistance from the latter.

The description of the two Bor-Hungary Death Marches graphically highlights the violence meted out. I do not know if my father was subject to violence by the guards during his march. What I do know is that Serbian villagers clearly watched the march.

What they saw was Jews being forced to march under armed guard, their physical condition clear to the naked eye. The "offer" of water reflects an understanding that help is needed; the "taunting" is but a manifestation of a deliberate physical, emotional, and existential degrading of another human being.

The villagers humiliated the marchers. More than that, their conscious decision not to provide assistance exacerbated already tenuous physical and emotional distresses.

The villagers' refusal to provide basic sustenance when *their* actions articulated recognition of the *need* for that very *sustenance* is the manifestation of a failure to act.

Holland

The five-year German occupation of Holland (1940–1945) is significantly distinct from the Death Marches. The differences are both in the duration of the relevant period and the nature of the preexisting relationship between the bystander and the victim.

The following suggests what was to come:

The violence began in February 1941. One evening, my grandfather came home with a swollen face and collapsed just inside the front door. He had been pulled off a tram and beaten up by a group of Dutch Nazis and their sympathizers. The family couldn't know that this was just one incident in a calculated campaign of terror organized by H. A. Rauter, the head of the SS campaign in the Netherlands. Gangs had been instructed to engage in just these kinds of random beatings and acts of vandalism, and the Dutch police were told not to intervene.[11]

The German occupation of Holland was marked by the deportation of an extraordinarily significant percentage of Dutch Jewry. The Dutch have benefited from favorable commentary regarding their treatment and protection of Dutch Jewry during World War II. However, subsequent historical research and their own recounting show this to be, largely, inaccurate.

The basis for the myth regarding widespread Dutch assistance to and rescue of Dutch Jewry is primarily, though not exclusively, based on the *Diary of Anne Frank*. Over the course of the decades, since its initial publication and in the aftermath of its remarkable worldwide success, an image was created of the Dutch heroically saving Holland Jewry.

Statistics strongly suggest this assumption factually incorrect; while reasons are varied and complex, understanding them is essential to the bystander discussion. In a conversation regarding a previous book project, former Dutch Minister of Justice Professor Hirsch Ballin made the following observation:

[W]e (the Dutch) are not a brave people though we have brave people.

Professor Ballin's insightful and thoughtful comment is particularly relevant to the bystander; as a matter of fact, it could be the subtitle of this book.

---

11. Rita Goldberg, *Motherland: Growing Up with the Holocaust*, Halban, London, 2014, pp. 64–65.

The failure of Dutch society to protect its Jewish population is one of the most troubling and tragic events in the Holocaust. The five-year German occupation of Holland met with minimal resistance led to the murder of 75 percent of Dutch Jewry. While this is not to suggest some members of Dutch society did not offer assistance and refuge, the fact that 75 percent of Dutch Jewry was murdered indicates the majority failed to save their fellow citizens.

Addressing the bystander question in the Netherlands focuses on individual and societal failure to assist the vulnerable over the course of an extended period of time. That is the essence of the relationship between Dutch Jews and their Gentile neighbors during the German occupation:

> *The Nazis raided the Jewish quarter on Saturday, February 22— the Sabbath—and again on Sunday, February 23. They rounded up 400 Jewish men, so-called hostages aged between twenty and thirty-five, in Jonas Daniel Meyer Square, the central point of the Jewish quarter. . . . . There were tourists around on Sunday, presumably from other parts of the city, who had come to gawk at the newly "picturesque" Jewish ghetto, and they too witnessed the extremely brutal arrests. The group of Jewish prisoners was sent first to Buchenwald and then to Mauthausen, supposedly to engage in hard labor. Only three young men survived. . . . . The rest of the Dutch group died within a few months of deportation.*[12]

Whether the ultimate fate of Dutch Jews was clear is a question of discussion and debate. Professor Bart van der Boom has addressed this question in his book, *"Wij weten niets van hun lot." Gewone Nederlanders en de Holocaust.*[13]

I have met with Professor van der Boom twice; our conversations have been immensely helpful, provocative, and engaging. Professor van der

---

12. Ibid., pp. 66–67.
13. Bart van der Boom, *"Wij weten niets van hun lot." Gewone Nederlanders en de Holocaust ("We know nothing of their fate." Ordinary Dutchmen and the Holocaust)*, Boom Geschiedenis, Amsterdam, the Netherlands, 2012.

Boom has been patient in answering my questions and gracious regarding my skepticism regarding his conclusions.

His book is based on an analysis of 194 diaries written during the Holocaust by Dutch Jews. It is, to the best of my knowledge, the only such published work. Based on "argument by the negative," van der Boom concludes that if diary writers did not note the fate that awaited them, that they did not know what fate awaited them seems to rely on assumption and conjecture.

I have shared with Professor van der Boom my skepticism regarding his argument; I am not convinced of the methodology's intellectual validity.

It is, in my opinion, an open question how much value historians can place in what diarists wrote and what larger conclusions can be drawn. However, based on my conversations with van der Boom, I do not accept the accusation that "whitewashing" Dutch compliance with the massive deportation of Dutch Jewry was his primary purpose.

Of that, I was not convinced in the least.

I have met with individuals who take umbrage at van der Boom; their criticism is both personal and professional. The most powerful complaint is that the book absolves Dutch society for its indifference to the plight of fellow citizens. In other words, van der Boom's analysis of the diaries acquits Gentiles for the fate of the Jews.

Cynically—more accurately, angrily—van der Boom's critics assert the primary question he posed, "how can you expect people to act when the victims did not know what awaited them," was framed in a manner intended to "close the book" on Dutch accommodation and acquiescence. In other words, victim ignorance justifies bystander nonaction. Victim ignorance equates to bystander innocence.

In some meetings, the anger expressed regarding van der Boom was visceral. At times, it was dismissive. It reflected a conviction his conclusion was not based on reasoned and measured analysis of the diaries.

I conveyed this to van der Boom; he was neither surprised nor particularly taken aback. My sense was that I was not telling him anything he did not know or recognize. His response was that he was honest to the diaries and could only read—and analyze—what the diarists themselves wrote 70 years ago. Even though I found his answer persuasive; I also understood the reactions of members of the Dutch Jewish community with whom I met.

His response was that of an author whose work is attacked.

The reaction to his book is deeply personal, reflecting decades-long questioning—and deep pain—regarding the deportation of 70 percent of Dutch Jewry. In many ways, I can relate to both van der Boom and his critics; both sides make compelling and convincing arguments.

Perhaps there is an element of truth in both arguments; perhaps their positions and conclusions are not mutually exclusive and the truth lies somewhere in the middle. However, what is clear is what the bystander observed.

To deny that Amsterdam's Gentile population saw Amsterdam's Jews disappearing in front of their eyes is the essence of the bystander who chooses not to look. It is not by chance that I use the word *physicality* to describe the Holocaust in general, and the bystander-victim relationship in particular.

The deportations—daily and nightly alike—were not occurring on the other side of the planet: Quite the opposite was taking place. They were happening across the street!

The deportations—the loading of Jews with their clothes, luggage, and families intact—were conducted in full view of their fellow citizens. This is particularly true with respect to the deportation of Dutch Jewry; it was important to maintain a façade of normalcy with minimal violence.

Doing so reflected the Nazi myth that Jews were being merely "relocated" to the East and therefore could travel with their suitcases. In large part, the deportations from Hungary—in spite of their late date—were similarly conducted. From the perspective of the bystander, then, the difference in the "visual" between deportations and Death Marches is stark.

By July 1942 the deportations had begun in earnest, not to end until September 1943, when the Netherlands was considered Judenrein, *Jew-free.*[14]

Simply put, neighbor turned his back on neighbor.

---

14. Goldberg, p. 76.

Hungary

In the course of three months, March to June 1944, 450,000 Hungarian Jews were deported, primarily to Auschwitz. The efficiency, speed, and single-mindedness with which Jews were deported was breathtaking.

Implementation of the Final Solution in Hungary—the massive deportation of Hungarian Jewry—received preference over providing arms to the Wehrmacht. In an extraordinary race against time, priority was given to the destruction of Hungarian Jewry. As the Red Army stood outside Budapest, Eichmann's efforts focused on the extermination of Hungarian Jewry, military consequences be damned.

German leadership largely understood Allied victory was all but inevitable. Nevertheless, expending extraordinary resources, for nonmilitary purposes, suggests fulfilling the Final Solution was more important than allocating resources to what was clearly becoming a desperate military effort.

Clearly, the deportation of Hungarian Jewry did not happen in a vacuum:

> *In 1938 the Hungarian parliament officially launched anti-Semitic legislation . . . a significant number of civil servants were ready to confront the Jews much more harshly than the parliament itself. During World War II this pressure—exerted by lower levels of the state upward and magnified by the Third Reich's increasing political influence and military power—continuously radicalized the climate and public discourse.*[15]
>
> *Measures exceeding the harsh provisions of anti-Semitic laws (in Hungary, ANG) were not only the results of local officials' tendency to try to radicalize the government's anti-Jewish policies . . . certain municipal bodies came up with complete plans to solve the 'Jewish question.'. . . after 1939, in all but a few large towns and cities, most Jewish representatives lost their membership in municipal bodies, and about 90% of Jewish citizens lost their right to vote.*[16]

---

15. Zoltan Vagi, Laszlo Csosz, and Gabor Kadar, *The Holocaust in Hungary: Evolution of a Genocide*, AltaMira Press, 2013, p. 23.
16. Ibid., p. 30.

In the words of Hungarian Minister of Defense Vilmos Nagybaczoni:

A few days after I assumed my duties, I already saw that the Jewish question was one of the toughest and gravest of problems that manifested all of its features within the army. . . . If someone had a conflict with a Jew, he would handle it by having that person called in for labor service, regardless of the person's age or social status.[17]

Unlike the five-year German occupation of Holland, Nazi control of Hungary was significantly shorter. Nevertheless, the consequences were tragically similar: 70 percent of Hungarian Jewry was killed in a remarkably short period of time.[18]

The rapidity with which Hungarian Jewry was deported—in the very late stages of the German war effort—is stunning. It reflects an extraordinary single-minded determination and focus.

Of Hungary, Mark Mazower writes:

The country they (German leadership, ANG) were most concerned about was Hungary, home of the largest Jewish community left in Europe. This was, of course, immediately endangered by the Wehrmacht's takeover in March 1944, and up to July 1944 more than 435,000 Hungarian Jews were sent to Auschwitz, far more than any other country. . . . The Hungarian transports thus marked the apogee of its murderous career. In May and June 1944 no fewer than one-third of the entire population of approximately one million people murdered there were killed.[19]

Deporting 450,000 Jews in a few short months requires extensive planning, ruthless execution, and profound cooperation from the larger public.

---

17. Vagi, Csosz, and Kadar, p. 52.
18. http://www.jewishvirtuallibrary.org/jsource/Holocaust/killedtable.html.
19. Mark Mazower, *Hitler's Empire: How the Nazi's Ruled Europe*, Penguin Books, New York, 2008, p. 404.

Anne Frank: What Do We Learn?

My mother survived the Holocaust in Budapest in circumstances similar to Anne Frank's. My connection—intellectual, emotional, and existential—to Anne Frank is so powerful that I dedicated one of my books, *Freedom from Religion: Rights and National Security*,[20] to her.

We will never know who "ratted out" Anne Frank and her family; we can but only guess at his or her motivation. Contrary to public myth, carefully cultivated over decades, the Netherlands had the highest percentage of collaborators of any nation occupied by the Nazis. As Daniel Goldhagen convincingly wrote in his pathbreaking work, *Hitler's Willing Executioners*, the Final Solution was dependent on local collaborators.[21]

Seeing is believing: A train trip from Budapest to eastern Hungary with my father crystallized, for me, the critical role individual Hungarians *must* have played in implementing the Final Solution in Hungary.

Without them, the Holocaust does not happen.

Restated: Without collaborators and bystanders, Hitler's Final Solution would have been a policy articulated but not implemented. The difference is the difference between life and death—between evil only imagined and evil actually carried out.

By collaborating, individuals may have saved their own lives and the lives of their families, but they surely sold their souls to the devil. The question is whether the fear of harm—to themselves and their families—as viable as it may have been, justifies, and excuses, their actions.

According to Yad Vashem, the Holocaust Memorial Museum in Jerusalem, over 25,000 Righteous Among the Nations from forty-four countries have been recognized for risking their lives in an effort to save Jews.[22]

We all make decisions—some larger, some smaller. Some decisions affect only ourselves. Some impact our loved ones and close friends. Others dramatically change the lives of people we do not know and might never meet.

---

20. Amos N. Guiora, *Freedom from Religion: Rights and National Security*, Oxford University Press, New York, 2009.

21. Daniel J. Goldhagen, *Hitler's Willing Executioners: Ordinary Germans and the Holocaust*, Knopf, New York, 1996.

22. http://www.yadvashem.org/yv/en/righteous/about.asp (last viewed November 13, 2015).

However, we are all accountable for our decisions and their impact. We bear, ultimately, individual responsibility and cannot—must not—hide behind the cloak of fear or umbrage from our community.

There is a difference between theoretical duress and actual duress; a defense predicated on *possible* harm either to the individual or his or her family is distinct from *directly* being forced to act.

By the same token, there is a difference between an individual crime—even murder—and a crime so widespread and so horrific that it can only be viewed as a crime against all mankind. Simply put, the defense of duress must be viewed in a limited, rather than broad, context.

Anne Frank stands for the challenges of decision making in times of existential crisis. She stands not just for the little girl hiding in the attic, but also for the person on the other side of the door who faces the decision of save or not save, protect or turn in.

Decisions are made daily; the question is what guides the decision maker. Even though there are innumerable factors involved, some decisions are black and white: Either you facilitate the knock on the door or you provide safe haven. Either you willingly participate in evil or you stand up and resist. Blurring, ultimately, facilitates evil.

— 5 —

The Bystander and the Victim

Who Is the Bystander?

As a reminder, I have defined the bystander as an individual who observes another in clear distress but is not the direct cause of the harm. A culpable bystander is one who has the ability to mitigate the harm but chooses not to.

Choosing the Holocaust as the frame of reference enabled me to understand the consequences of bystander nonaction when governments, state agents, and anti-Semitism joined forces to kill 6 million Jews.

Examining my parents' Holocaust experiences enabled me to understand the consequences of the bystander on a deeply personal level. Focus on my parents enabled transition from the abstract to the concrete.

That transition was of the utmost importance. What began as a question of academic inquiry became an issue that went far beyond mere discourse. The challenge was—and is—to propose legislation that makes bystander nonaction a crime.

Failure to intervene on behalf of a readily identifiable victim will be a crime in accordance with jurisdictionally relevant criminal codes. The determining point of inquiry is whether the bystander had the ability to mitigate harm to another but failed to do so.

That is distinct from a civil action in which an aggrieved individual files a lawsuit against another person. My proposal is not a tort action between two persons, rather a criminal action brought by the state against a wrongdoer.

The wrongdoer is the bystander who failed to provide assistance. I propose that nonintervention be defined a crime. It raises innumerable questions. Those questions focus on the extent to which the state can regulate individual conduct and impose the social contract on the body politic. Those concerns are understandable.

However, the primary lesson of the Holocaust is that silence in the face of evil enables and enhances its inevitable consequences. That is the direct result of complicity. Bystanders who observed my parents—in different locations and distinct cultural and social circumstances—were complicit in the harm perpetrators imposed on them.

There are, obviously, distinct categories of bystanders; it is incorrect to "lump" them into one class, devoid of differentiation and nuance. That is in accordance with basic criminal law principles weighing circumstances, capabilities, age, education, and prior history. The bystander must be in a position to directly observe, assess, and act.

Social media has impacted the physical presence requirement; electronic communication has significantly broadened the scale and scope of bystanders. I can sit in my living room, receive pictures of a victim in distress thousands of miles away, and with a click of my keyboard immediately alert relevant officials and the larger public—regardless of where I am and regardless of where the victim is. That is the reality of social media, whether Facebook, text messages, Instagram, or other means of immediate communication. However, I do not believe that criminal liability can be imposed on the bystander via social media.

I have given this question much thought. There is no easy answer. However, after careful consideration—with the understanding that both positions are reasonable—my proposed model is limited to the bystander being *physically* present. Physicality is essential to imposing criminal liability on the bystander who fails to act.

That is very different from the social media bystander dependent on communication from others who, themselves, may, or may not, be physically present. The social media bystander is, for me, too removed and distant to bear criminal liability for nonaction.

Perhaps, by analogy, it is akin to hearsay evidence that, subject to exceptions, is inadmissible in a court of law. Because pictures can be Photoshopped, selectively taken, and shared, the lack of physical immediacy significantly impacts assigning liability for bystander nonintervention.

It is that physicality that enables the bystander to see and sense, in an unfiltered manner, the distress of the victim. The *physically present bystander* may choose to deliberately ignore the victim's need for help, but it is well nigh impossible for that bystander to claim, "I didn't see."

On that note, a thoughtful reader suggests the social contract, as traditionally understood, is between the state and the individual rather than between individuals. Although there is much merit to the suggestion, it reflects a limited understanding of the relationship-obligation between individuals who are members of similar contractual relationships.

There are, then, two social contracts relevant to the bystander discussion—between the individual and nation-state and among individuals.

My proposal imposes on the individual *the responsibility* to act on behalf of another individual and subsequently grants the state *the power* to prosecute for nonintervention.

Complicity

Were all bystanders complicit? No. Could all bystanders to my parents' distress have assisted them? No. For that reason, visits to Holland, Germany, and Hungary were essential; the only way I could truly understand the physicality of the bystander-victim relationship was to sit, walk, and stand in the footsteps of the Holocaust.

There is, nevertheless, danger in my decision to examine the bystander through the Holocaust; after all, individuals were brutalized, beaten, and murdered by a regime whose essence was fear, intimidation, and violence.

In other words, goes the argument, violence was state sanctioned, anti-Semitism was legislated, and the rule of law was brutally discarded. How is it possible, I am asked, to expect anyone to "stand up and do the right thing" when the raison d'etre of the state is murder of Jews?

That, after all, is the crux of the decision reached at Wannsee. The murderers and their collaborators were but implementing government policies; bystanders were but observing state-sanctioned violence. The former were carrying out orders; the latter were primarily focused on their survival and safety.

The social contract between individuals and the state was violently broken; any sense of social contract between individuals took a back seat to the brutal designation, by the state, of Jews as "enemies."

The argument is compelling, perhaps even convincing. It is neat and tidy. It excuses individual nonaction under the guise of "state action." Jews were legitimate targets; therefore, all action taken against them was lawful.

In the traditional duty-to-act model, preexisting relationships significantly impact the obligation requirement. A parent has a special duty with respect to his or her child; an individual, with no preexisting relationship or devoid of special responsibility, does not have the equivalent duty to act.

In practical terms, the bystander—in accordance with the definition above—is the individual who does not have a special relationship with or obligation to the victim. Our focus is on that very individual; the individual who saw the Death Marches and watched Jews being humiliated, beaten, and murdered.

We know he saw; we know she observed. That is a reality, perhaps uncomfortable, albeit undeniable. Limited conversations with my parents highlighted how obvious their distress was. Villagers saw my father on his Death March.

Budapest residents saw my mother and grandmother—wearing the readily visible Yellow Star—going from safe house to safe house. Holocaust literature proves the plight of Jews known—potential danger clear, vulnerability apparent.

What Is Required of the Bystander?

Reservations regarding imposition of criminal liability for failure to act raise philosophical and practical questions. One reader, a very thoughtful Israeli, asked me the following question: Do I believe

Israelis who oppose Israeli government policy in the West Bank and Gaza Strip are bystanders for failing to intervene on behalf of Palestinians?

That question has been asked of me more than once. It is an important question for it goes to the heart of determining who is a bystander and how I intend to apply my proposed definition. My focus is exclusively on the bystander whose physical proximity to the victim is immediate.

The individual who reads a newspaper, writes blogs, and discusses vexing social and political issues with family members is an abstract bystander. That person is not physically present and therefore not in a position to immediately act. That is not to say that concerned members of the public should not write letters to the editor, participate in demonstrations, and express their opinions freely and openly. However, they do not meet the bystander test as I propose.

In the Palestinian-Israeli context, an Israeli living in Tel Aviv does not have a direct relationship, whether short term or long term, with a Palestinian living in the West Bank.

That Israeli, unquestionably, has an abstract relationship—as a citizen of Israel—with Palestinians living in the West Bank. After all, the Israeli government exercises powers, responsibilities, and authority in the West Bank, thereby directly impacting Palestinians living in the West Bank. And that Israeli can demonstrate in the public square, vote for the opposition political party, and otherwise express opposition to government policy.

The bystander model I am proposing is predicated on a "one-to-one" relationship between bystander and victim. That is distinct from highly noteworthy and commendable efforts intended to save broad categories of individuals, including victims of natural disasters and starving children.

The Serbian villager who saw my father on his Death March in late September 1944 was not thousands of miles away; he was not disengaged, sitting in his living room reading accounts of Death Marches.

That villager witnessed my father's Death March.

That villager willfully ignored my father's distress in an hour of enormous need. That villager—in immediate physical proximity to my father—is the classic bystander, literally right there, able to offer water, food, or a blanket.

In choosing not to, regardless of whether initially taunting my father or not, the bystander deliberately chose not to intervene. That decision was, doubtlessly, based on a variety of decision points.

In the model I propose, the bystander must have the ability to save a *specific* victim rather than a *class* of victims. The paradigm I am advocating is premised on the bystander who is physically present and capable of intervening on behalf of a specific victim.

The requirement is that the bystander *sees* a specific individual in distress. However, in order to minimize possible harm to the bystander, the action requirement does not require actual physical intervention. Physicality of the setting is of the utmost importance.

The physicality as I observed in Amsterdam and Berlin lends itself to a direct and intimate relationship between victim and bystander. In that intimacy, the bystander directly observes the condition, circumstance, and distress of the victim.

Regardless whether the victim is my mother, my father, a rape victim, or a specific war refugee, the bystander has become, whether intended or not, engaged in a relationship with that person. That relationship, regardless of whether bystander and victim had a preexisting relationship, imposes on the bystander the obligation to act.

In this proposed model, the action requirement can be met, in the contemporary age, by calling the police and informing them of a particular crisis. It is sufficient to provide basic information that will enable first responders to act in accordance with their professional training and judgment.

There is no requirement that the bystander physically intervene. Rather, the action that would satisfy the legal test I am proposing is twofold—recognizing an individual is in distress and notifying the relevant authorities. However, imposition of bystander liability is predicated on the ability to provide concrete assistance to the victim.

Mitigating circumstances—particularly related to age and ability—are to be factored. However, the minimal requirement of alerting authorized authorities largely negates the "threat to bystander" concern traditionally raised when duty-to-act laws are discussed.

Victims

A crime requires a victim. There must be an individual who is harmed, whether physically or otherwise. In the Holocaust, victims of the Nazi regime were humiliated, brutalized, and murdered.

I have thought a great deal about how the victim perceived the bystander. In particular, I have asked whether the victim had any expectation of the bystander. That has become, in the context of this book, an overwhelmingly important point of inquiry.

In addition to looking at countless Holocaust pictures, I have spent hours looking at grainy black-and-white film capturing painful images from the Holocaust. My attention is drawn to the victim. The pictures are painful but instructive.

The more I watch, the more it is clear just how alone the victim was. That is true whether in the selection line in Auschwitz, in the labor camps, hiding in the attic in Budapest, being brutalized in the streets of Poland, or being shot in Lithuania.

However, the victim was not really alone. After all, fellow citizens were observing or beating. The victim is looking at both the nonintervening bystander and the brutalizing perpetrator. In many instances, all three are citizens of the same country and yet one has been defined as the "enemy." That designation justifies beating, if not death.

For me, looking at Holocaust pictures, contemplating the distress of the victim, the "expectation" question is of primary importance. That question is relevant regardless of whether a preexisting relationship existed or not. My parents did not have expectations of the bystanders who observed them.

There is no way of knowing whether my grandparents—as they walked from their modest home to the train station—had any thoughts regarding their fellow townspeople. Perhaps because they lived a largely Jewish life, separated from Gentiles, they had no expectations. In that sense, perhaps the Gentiles were total strangers to my grandparents—people with whom they had no previous contact or interaction.

It is not an abstract inquiry: The question, and its consequences, is very real for me.

Train Platforms

A few years ago I was invited by the German military to meet with senior officers on an unrelated matter. The German officer who initiated the invitation contacted me regarding travel logistics. He suggested we meet at the train station platform outside the Frankfurt Airport.

I instinctively replied we do not meet as he suggests, rather meet elsewhere at the airport. Without questioning me, he graciously agreed. At the end of my three-day stay in Germany, while we were drinking a beer, he asked me why I had so responded.

My answer was clear and direct: "The last time your people invited my people to meet at the train station it didn't work out so well." He looked at me, thought for a second, and said: "I had never thought about it that way."

I believed him, without hesitation. In recounting this story many times, I have always emphasized his response was genuine. I truly believe his invitation to meet at the platform was predicated on convenience and basic logistical considerations.

That, however, was not how I viewed the suggested meeting location. For me, the "train platform" has unique meaning, practically and emotionally. I have looked at innumerable pictures of Jews standing at train platforms with guards about to push them onto trains. The scene represents the last minutes of their world, as they knew it. Their death was all but guaranteed the moment the train door closed behind them.

For me, the picture of the Jew standing on the platform is akin to the condemned about to walk to the gallows. There is, of course, one critical difference. The condemned knows death is imminent and has had an opportunity to prepare for impending demise; the Jew does not know for certain where the train is headed and what fate waits.

Perhaps there are assumptions, speculations, fears, and foreboding. These are victims whose deaths have been ordered in accordance with the Final Solution; the guards will shortly order them to board the train, and then they will close the doors. In the meantime, bystanders stand and watch as their former neighbors, professional colleagues, and erstwhile acquaintances are pushed ever closer to their deaths.

In all likelihood they had stood on that platform countless times previously. Never had they stood there about to embark on their final destination—one they had no control over, predetermined to result in their brutal murder. The pictures are uniformly similar: They show families with their suitcases, well dressed, looking around them, surrounded by armed soldiers and citizens loitering in their vicinity.

When the train arrives at Auschwitz, guards will open the doors and order the Jews to "selection lines" where their fate will be decided within minutes. Those chosen for the gas chamber—as was the case with my grandparents—will die immediately; others will be spared, temporarily, and sent to work battalions. Efficiency and speed were of maximum priority; Jews sent to the gas chambers did not receive a number and were not tattooed, unlike those selected for work.[1]

Train platform pictures are very different from images of brutal humiliation and murder in the streets of Europe. The train platform pictures depict orderliness; street pictures depict soldiers and civilians brutalizing their Jewish victims. *In both situations, the victim was clearly identified and specially targeted.*

The attacker—whether soldier and/or civilian—fully intended the harm inflicted. That is the essence of the perpetrator. An extraordinary killing machine was established by Nazi Germany. It was efficient, brutal, unrelenting, and unforgiving. The term *madness* has been applied to Nazi Germany: I find the term inappropriate and deceiving.

Germany

The victim discussion requires examining Germany distinct from Holland and Hungary. The reason is obvious: Germany bears ultimate responsibility for the murder of 6 million Jews.

Nazi sympathizers and collaborators throughout Europe are, also—without doubt—guilty for their role in implementation of the Final Solution.

---

1. http://www.ushmm.org/wlc/en/article.php?ModuleId=10007056.

Nevertheless, regardless of how violent, brutal, and murderous they were, there is an important distinction between the Dutch collaborator and the German Nazi. The former were implementers; the latter were planners. That is a significant difference.

A German scholar shared with me his family was "also a victim." When I inquired as to details, his response was that "the allies bombed my grandparents' farm in southern Germany." I have no reason to doubt him. I am also confident the bombing attack caused financial damage and hardship to the family.

However, I find his stake to victimhood to be a stretch. The fate that awaited my grandparents when they were deported to Auschwitz is very different from Allied bombing of southern Germany. The decision to exterminate European Jewry is distinct from strategic decisions regarding military targets.

The killing of my grandparents was deliberate. By any definition, they were, doubtlessly, intended victims. That is not to be confused with whatever economic harm befell German farmers whose land was bombed by the Allies during a six-year-long war started by Germany.

Targeting German farms reflected military strategy; the impact on the particular farmer—whether financial or injury or death—was not aimed at that farmer. The Allies did not declare war on German farmers; in direct contrast, the Final Solution reflected Nazi Germany's race theories, specifically aimed at exterminating European Jewry. The Jews were the specific targets.

Conversely, the Allies' war efforts focused on defeating a nation-state. A heavy price was exacted on Germany's civilian population. The "carpet bombing" of Dresden, February 1945, is a striking example of Allied efforts and measures. Seventy years later, the bombing is controversial regarding international law principles including proportionality and collateral damage.

Regardless of important academic discourse on this subject, the damage—and undeniable harm—can be directly attributed to the German regime that initiated the war with support of its civilian population. How deep and wide the support is a matter of debate among historians.

A significant percentage of the population enthusiastically responded to Hitler's aggressive military posture and actions. Hitler was largely unopposed by the mid-1930s; the German public rallied around the loud, violent, and consistent beating of war drums.

Similarly, the German public did not exhibit—explicitly or implicitly—significant push-back to the regime's racial policies. The increasingly strident anti-Semitism marked by legislation intended to exclude Jews from civil life and to define "Jews as enemy" was met with widespread support, but not absolute support as evidenced by significant resistance to Nazi calls to boycott Jewish stores. The regime's decision to reverse course and cancel the boycott suggests decision makers were very attuned to public opinion and how particular measures were perceived.

Richard Evans has used the words "intimidation," "fear," and "terror" to describe the relationship between the public and the regime. That, however, does not satisfactorily explain the enthusiasm with which the German public embraced Hitler's vicious anti-Semitism.

Leni Riefenstahl brilliantly and vividly captured the raw emotion and seemingly insatiable adulation for, and support of, the regime in her movie, *Triumph of the Will*.[2] The two-pronged effort of the Nazi regime—conquering Europe and exterminating European Jewry—required both decisive and committed leadership and broad public support in Germany.

Maintenance of the extraordinary effort that demanded unparalleled resources, manpower, and focus significantly benefited from identifying Jews as "the enemy." Blaming world Jewry for Germany's defeat in World War I, the rise of the Weimar Republic and its inevitable ills enabled Hitler to coalesce public opinion around an easily identifiable, common enemy. That theme was present throughout the twelve-year reign of the Third Reich. It was essential for implementation of the Final Solution.

The incessant repetition of "Jew as enemy" ensured institutionalization of Jews as victims; it was a deliberate effort to rally the German public. Kristallnacht was but the most visible and violent prewar manifestation of the regime's obsession with German Jewry. It sent a loud and clear message regarding the fate that awaited Jews.

Unfortunately, many failed to understand or refused to read the proverbial tea leaves. Jews were particularly targeted for they were the clearly

---

2. https://www.youtube.com/watch?v=GHs2coAzLJ8.

identified enemy and therefore the specific victim. All that followed was application of the public's embrace of Hitler speeches, warnings, and leadership.

The result was, in retrospect, clear: Jews were identified as legitimate targets.

Nuance

Nuance is important; perhaps things are not always as they seem on the surface. Three stories are particularly relevant. I have been granted permission to share the stories below on condition of anonymity.

Story 1 (as told to me by a Dutch friend)
In Amsterdam, during the deportations of Dutch Jewry, his mother allowed a young woman (it is unclear whether she was Jewish) to enter her home in the evening. This occurred in the hours when the curfew was in effect.

My friend's grandfather was in a position of authority in the Dutch government that relocated to London with the Queen in May 1940; the Germans held my friend's father in a concentration camp.

The mother conditioned the invitation: The young woman must leave in the morning, even though she did not have an alternative hiding place.

What was the reason for the "condition"?

My friend's mother was concerned harm would befall her husband would it be discovered she had given shelter to the young woman.

My friend told me this story over a wonderful dinner. He is proud of his mother for taking the young woman in and understands why, in the morning, she asked her to leave. He does not see a contradiction between the two.

To this day, he does not know if the young woman survived the war. He does not believe his mother was a bystander as I have defined it.

Quite the opposite; he is politely adamant she did the best under very difficult circumstances as harm to her detained husband was a very real possibility. While providing temporary relief, her primary focus was on her family.

Story 2 (as written to me by a Dutch friend)

From the stories my mother told me, my grandmother provided shelter to a Jewish woman and her two children in the war. They did not know each other before. My grandfather was fighting in the resistance and was captured by the Germans and transported to Germany to work in a camp.

They had two sons and my mother (born in 1941). They were not bystanders in my opinion.

My grandmother was on her own with a husband captured and could not cope with the pressure anymore. Therefore, she asked the resistance to find the woman and the children another place.

She always felt guilty about that, but I must admit I am proud she did it, even if only for a while.

Taking into account the consequences for her own three little children, I do understand her decision.

I think it would have made a difference if she had known the woman or was friendly with her beforehand.

My friend had briefly shared this story with me when we met for a drink when I began researching this book. When I asked her to put the story in writing she did so graciously.

There is no doubt my friend feels great pride in her grandmother's taking in the woman and children and also fully understands the decision to ask them to leave.

Both friends are deeply respectful of the respective decisions made; in both cases, there is pride mixed with understanding of the dilemma's complexity. The desire to protect family members is, understandably, uppermost in the decision-making process.

Both friends rejected the suggestion that their mother and grandmother were bystanders. Rather, both felt a balance—under extremely difficult circumstances—was struck even though the decision may have resulted in the deaths of the Jews.

Conversely, it is not unreasonable to assume that, given the extraordinarily high deportation rate of Dutch Jewry to Auschwitz, death may have been the inevitable result under any condition.

I shared both stories with my mother.

She well understood the actions of the mother and grandmother. She did not fault either for requesting the Jews leave even though they had no clear alternative hiding place. She understood the need to protect their family members, even though asking the women to leave clearly endangered them.

Doubtlessly, both the mother and grandmother well understood the possible consequences of their respective actions. For my friends—and mother—that did not outweigh the courageousness of the initial decision to provide haven.

My mother fully appreciated the primary responsibility of both women was the welfare of their family members.

Friends in the United States and Israel with whom I have shared both vignettes agree with my mother. The response has, largely, been two-fold—laudatory regarding the decision to provide haven, regardless of the length of time, and uncertainty regarding how they, themselves, would act in similar circumstances.

Both vignettes highlight the extraordinary tenuousness and uncertainty of the victim. Those willing to assist are burdened with considerations extending beyond the immediate needs of the victim. While the victim is in danger, offers of assistance are, as these examples highlight, not "cost free." That, of course, does not mitigate the situation for the victim.

Perhaps the opposite is true as the dilemma of a potential rescuer accentuates the direness of the victim's situation.

Story 3

There is, of course, a different perspective brought to light by the following story. It is, sadly, a tragedy. Its importance is that it highlights different standards of conduct and their consequences, whether intended or not.

I met with a Dutch Holocaust survivor, who graciously welcomed me to her home and offered me coffee and cookies.

In advance of our meeting I sent her a list of questions intended to serve as a basis for our conversation. She was four years old when the Germans occupied Holland; seven when she, her parents, and her three-and-a-half-year-old brother went into hiding.

There is a painful aspect of the decision to go into hiding: KS's grand-parents did not join the family and were deported to Auschwitz where they were murdered. The grandparents did not go into hiding as the Dutch resistance—responsible for "matching" Dutch Jews with Gentiles who offered their homes for hiding—gave clear preference to younger people.

KS described to me in vivid—and painful—detail the moment she, her brother, and her parents took leave of their grandparents with whom they had lived after May 1940 when the Germans occupied Holland.

The family went into hiding at nighttime once the curfew went into effect.

They traveled by train from their city of residence to the town where they would live in hiding. To the best of her recollection there were no bystanders watching them walk to the train station. At the train station, she recalls soldiers and policemen but not civilians.

When the train stopped, men KS believes to have been members of the Resistance met them. As was the case with others, her family went into hiding in three separate houses: Her parents stayed together; her brother went to a second house; and she went to a third house.

The three houses were in the same community; however, there was no physical contact between the children and their parents during the hiding period. She and her parents were able to communicate by letter writing; the Dutch resistance, who made all transportation and hiding arrangements for the family, delivered the letters.

KS who "looked Aryan" was able to go to school while in hiding; she was introduced as the family's cousin and did not raise suspicion among neighbors, teachers, and friends.

One day she received a letter from her mother expressing anxiety regarding her brother's condition; the mother's concern was based on the content of letters she received from the people who were purportedly hiding the brother. Her "maternal instinct" proved correct; the people had left their house, thereby abandoning the child.

The Dutch resistance moved him to a different home. Shortly thereafter, the authorities came to the second house and demanded the brother be given to them. From there he was taken to the local police station, then transferred to Westerbork[3] and ultimately deported to Auschwitz where he was murdered. The parents were informed of his fate after the war when they were reunited with KS.

KS's story is painful; of that, there is no doubt. When she showed me two pictures of her brother—one from a family portrait, the other taken by a Red Cross nurse at Westerbork—the question of complicity was uppermost in my mind.

I requested to know how the child was "outed." In other words, as was the case with my mother in Budapest, the question of who "snitched" to the authorities was of great importance to me.

The question is at the heart of the complicity discussion this book addresses. It goes to the core of M's question regarding, "how did this happen"; it raises important issues regarding the resistance-collaboration-postwar "account settling"; it is essential to categorization of participants; and it is highly relevant to victim expectation.

KS shared with me her brother was "outed" by a woman who had a quarrel with the family hiding the child. That quarrel resulted in the child's murder in Auschwitz. I was intrigued whether accounts were settled after the war; KS did not share my conviction this would have been justified. We agreed to disagree.

This woman was not a bystander; she was a participant in the fullest sense of the word. Even though she was not an official, Dutch or German, her actions directly led to the child's murder. That is distinct from the bystander whose complicity is defined by a failure to intervene.

However, from the victim's perspective, the result is oftentimes the same—harm, if not death.

The woman was actively responsible for the child's murder; she went well beyond the nonintervention that marked the conduct of villagers

---

3. http://www.ushmm.org/wlc/en/article.php?ModuleId=10005217.

observing my father's Death March. Those observing were the classic bystanders; this woman clearly crossed the boundary between bystander and participant. Her guilt is obvious; convincing the reader of their guilt is essential to assigning criminal liability for nonintervention.

In both cases, the vulnerable victim is just that, vulnerable and abandoned.

In assigning guilt, that reality is of primary importance.

Fragility: Expectation versus Obligation

Recognizing the rescuer's dilemma—"what are the consequences if I act?"—is essential to understanding the victim's precariousness. The fact that there are potentially significant costs associated with providing assistance highlights victim fragility.

That fragility is doubtlessly magnified when extraordinary state resources are dedicated to destruction of an entire class of specific victims. The overwhelming failure of civilians to provide assistance enhanced the destruction of European Jewry.

The victim, clearly visible by the Yellow Star, was targeted for death by the racist policies of the Nazi regime and abandoned by fellow citizens. In many cases, fellow citizens were willing participants in the implementation of the Final Solution.

However, it is the theme and consequences of "abandonment" that weighs heavily on my mind. Whether predicated on anti-Semitism, fear of being perceived as providing a haven to the enemy, or other motivations is a matter for historical and psychological conjecture.

Whatever the explanation, the *consequences* from the victim's perspective are obvious and painful. They are also, unfortunately, predictable and repetitive. That is, regardless of circumstances, victim vulnerability is, tragically, a recurring theme in the face of perpetrator violence and bystander complicity.

To appreciate the consequences of complicity requires understanding vulnerability and abandonment.

The Holocaust is an extreme example of victim distress. That, however, should not minimize societal recognition of the costs incurred by victims in other situations and circumstances. The gist of the Final Solution should not distract us from the daily reality of victims in contemporary society.

The victim can be anyone, whether specifically targeted or the classic "wrong place, wrong time" unintended victim. Both—intended and unintended—are deserving of protection. In the context of the bystander, protection is best ensured if intervention is a legal obligation.

While writing this chapter I received a particularly insightful and thoughtful email articulating concerns regarding my proposal. The writer, while sympathetic to the effort, was skeptical regarding legislation requiring bystander intervention.

Conversation with my running partner after receiving the email led to the title of this section. I adopted M's recommendation without hesitation for it concisely captured the crux of the dilemma: Do we rely on an individual's knowing the right thing to do, or do we impose on the bystander the obligation to act.

From the victim's perspective, decisive action mitigating actual harm is of the essence. Relying on a moral code is insufficient; imposing legal liability is essential. The analysis must be through the lens of the victim.

The victim—intended and unintended alike—is dependent on intervention; that dependence represents the fragility of the vulnerable individual. Fragility and vulnerability are the crux of being a victim, whether on a Death March, in a present-day refugee camp in Europe, or at a college fraternity party where "date rape" drugs are common.

One of the most important questions regarding the victim is expectation of assistance: Is it reasonable to expect someone, anyone, will intervene on your behalf? That question weighed heavily on my mind in limited conversations with my parents.

Both emphasized they had no expectation of assistance from bystanders. They made that very clear. For them, bystander assistance was well beyond the realm of the possible. It was something they dismissed outright in our discussions. I was struck by their immediate rejection of the concept: Their dismissal was not mixed with anger, rather it reflected acceptance of the historical circumstances of Jews in Hitler's Europe.

That, for me, heightened the sense of abandonment I assumed they felt as victims. The sense of being alone in the face of attack—physical, verbal, or impending—is a disturbingly powerful victim motif. Even though the range of victims covers a wide spectrum, there are common themes irrespective of circumstances and conditions. I found myself asking whether loneliness and abandonment is the reality of victims with no expectation of intervention on their behalf.

If that is an accurate assessment, then victim vulnerability, in the face of perpetrator violence compounded by no expectation of assistance, is a deep stain on society—regardless of which society, regardless of whom the bystander is, and regardless of whom the perpetrator is.

The question of victim expectation weighs heavily on my mind. I find myself looking at pictures of Holocaust and non-Holocaust victims alike. I try to focus on what they are looking at. I try to understand their mindset at the moment when their very being is at risk—not tomorrow, today. As my focus is the bystander-victim relationship, I am only interested in the latter's expectation of the former.

Is the victim's expectation of assistance reasonable? For the victim, it is essential—perhaps lifesaving—but the query is whether *relying* on someone "stepping forward" is a reasonable expectation. I believe it is not.

It is for that reason, as the title of this subsection suggests, that *expectation needs to be replaced by obligation.* Assistance must be forthcoming; time is of the essence. The focal point is the victim's immediate, potential danger; failure to understand that dramatically enhances victim vulnerability.

— 6 —

The Crime of Complicity

Defining Complicity and Dangers of Imposing Liability on Bystanders

The question of complicity is essential to determining bystander liability. I define complicity as an act that furthers a crime committed by another. Professor Sanford Kadish, writing in 1985, suggested the following definition:

> [T]he doctrine of complicity (sometimes referred to as the law of aiding and abetting, or accessorial liability) emerges to define the circumstances in which one person (to whom I will refer as the secondary party or actor, accomplice, or accessory) becomes liable for the crime of another (the primary party or actor, or the principal).[1]

The person who is complicit has failed to make reasonable efforts to prevent a crime; that failure is tantamount to the crime of nonintervention. The difference between the perpetrator and the complicit bystander is significant.

---

1. Sanford H. Kadish, Complicity, cause and blame: A study in the interpretation of doctrine, *California Law Review*, 73(2), 1985, p. 336.

The complicit individual is not the perpetrator; the two actors do not bear similar liability given profound differences between them. The perpetrator is the aggressor, actively acting against the victim; the complicit individual is liable for failure to act.

That crime is predicated on passivity. Rather than taking measures to minimize or mitigate potential harm, the bystander failed the victim. Whether standing and watching or walking away, deliberately oblivious to harm posed to another, the bystander is complicit.

What about risks to the bystander, I am repeatedly asked. Might the perpetrator not harm the intervening bystander? Why should the bystander risk life and limb or endanger family members on behalf of another? Perhaps an altercation is not what it seems: Perhaps the victim instigated and the seeming perpetrator is responding in justifiable self-defense.

These are legitimate questions; they correctly cast doubt regarding the proposition that bystander nonintervention justifies initiation of criminal process by the state. After all, goes the argument: How can the state demand a bystander intervene when intervention may harm the bystander, or family members?

Is that not an undue burden to impose on an individual unacquainted with perpetrator and victim alike? Why should an individual who has no connection to a situation unfolding in front of him or her be required to act?

The criticism, in a nutshell, is this: Requiring intervention when circumstances are unclear and the unfolding situation is uncertain and shrouded in murkiness is to impose an unreasonable duty on the bystander. In other words, the state would be deliberately endangering innocent members of society.

The counterarguments to my proposal are almost persuasive. They are well thought out, logical in their criticism, reasonable, and understandable. It is, without doubt, no mean thing to demand individuals intervene on behalf of a victim. Especially one they have never met and know nothing about.

In the Holocaust, Jews were defined as "enemies of the state"; they were ghettoized and deported by the state. Why should anyone provide assistance to an individual that government has deliberately sought to castigate, separate from society, and demonize?

Complicity directly contributes to victim harm; the failure to intervene on behalf of the vulnerable is the essence of the bystander. It is the exact opposite of what Martha Minow defines as the upstander;[2] rather than, as Dean Minow suggests, "doing the right thing," the bystander chooses inaction and nonintervention.

It is that nonintervention—regardless of motivation—that makes the bystander complicit. The burden, from a legal perspective, is defining the contours of bystander and complicity alike.

Casual observation of clear harm to another combined with a failure to minimize that harm makes the observer complicit in that harm. The critical word is *harm*; the question is what does it mean to be complicit and how is the term to be applied?

In assessing whether the crime of complicity was committed, it is essential to focus, with great specificity, on the actions—or, more correctly, the inactions—of the bystander. Not all bystanders carry the same weight of guilt.

The determining factors in assessing complicity include physical proximity to the victim, clarity of the situation, capability of providing assistance, degree of assistance required, and degree of risk intervention implies. Those five, individually and collectively, determine whether the bystander was complicit.

The Crime of Complicity

Implementation of the Final Solution—the deliberate, conscious decision to eradicate European Jewry—required something else. That extra, for lack of a better term, was the complicity of millions throughout Europe. While the Third Reich created policy, its implementation was dependent on two additional actors—perpetrators and bystanders.

The perpetrators are too numerous to count—Lithuanians who shot Jews, Latvians who forced Jews to dig their own graves, Ukrainians who brutalized Jews, Germans who gassed Jews in concentration camps, Polish

---

2. Martha Minow, *Upstanders, Whistle-Blowers, and Rescuers*, Koningsberger Lecture delivered on December 13, 2014, Utrecht University, the Netherlands.

train conductors who transported Jews to Auschwitz, Dutch policemen who rounded up Jews, Hungarian Arrow Cross who murdered Jews, and French authorities who collaborated with the German occupation.

As long and reprehensible as that list is—and it is but a sample of European perpetrators—it does not fully explain the murder of 6 million Jews. To fully understand the Final Solution requires us to recognize the complicity of the bystander. To what extent Heydrich assumed bystander complicity when establishing the Final Solution is unclear; what is clear is the degree to which bystander complicity enabled the Final Solution.

That is, perpetrator conduct was the active "engine" that drove the Holocaust, whereas bystander nonintervention was essential to its implementation. That nonintervention is the complicity that enabled perpetrators to fulfill Hitler's goal of destroying European Jewry. Without their complicity, the Holocaust does not occur on the scale it did; that same refrain is relevant to crimes, whether large or small, committed in the decades after the Holocaust.

For that reason I recommend bystander complicity be understood to be a crime. For some, framing bystander complicity as a "moral code" is comforting and more tolerable than defining it as a crime. Doing so resonates with notions of acting ethically in the face of aggression to another. There is something reassuring in convincing ourselves we "know the right thing to do."

However, the *aspirational* model is just that, aspirational. The reality—as uncomfortable as it may be—is that the "doing the right thing" is, largely, illusionary, reflecting empty words. Bystander complicity is more common than bystander intervention; turning the proverbial blind eye far outweighs standing up to violence exercised by another.

History clearly shows that, unfortunately.

Because harm is the direct result of bystander nonintervention, complicity must be perceived as directly contributing to that harm.

The term *complicit*, in this context, is neither abstract nor philosophical; it is intended from a purely legal perspective with consequences to the actor. The culpable actor is the one who failed to act; the crime committed was nonintervention.

Nonintervention is the essence of complicity. With respect to bystander complicity, the focus is assistance *not* provided by the bystander to the victim in the face of clear and present danger posed by the perpetrator. The bystander fails to intervene on behalf of a vulnerable individual. That makes the bystander complicit regarding harm that befalls the victim.

However, casting too broad a net is unreasonable and unfeasible. Similarly, unnecessarily limiting application of the proposed bystander definition would fail to achieve my stated goal.

The burden is applying a legally tolerable and practically implementable definition. The former requires a definition that squares with accepted due process and equal protection standards; the latter requires a definition that enables reasonable application of prosecutorial discretion.

There is no intention or benefit proposing a definition that will be cast asunder by prosecutors. That would be self-defeating. The focus is on the individual physically present where harm is occurring who chooses not to intervene.

The bystander's nonintervention reflects a conscious, deliberate rationale-based decision to avoid involvement in the face of harm to another individual. Liability is dependent on ascertaining the bystander was in a position to provide assistance. It is a fact-based determination. Nuance and circumstances are essential in determining whether the particular bystander, potentially a defendant in a criminal action initiated by the state, was in a position to intervene and thereby mitigate victim harm.

The consequences, from the bystander's perspective, are significant. Unlike moral judgment assessing whether the individual "did the right thing," imposition of criminal liability reflects the state's assessment that the individual has committed a crime. That is very different from moral judgment; the consequences from the individual's perspective are, potentially, significant.

The decision to prosecute for the failure to intervene reflects society's acknowledgment that relying on individual moral codes and ethical judgments is, unfortunately, unwarranted. Requiring—by power of the law—an individual to intervene on behalf of another reflects recognition that the power and pull of morality is, ultimately, limited.

The Talmud teaches us "whoever saves a life, it is considered as if he saved an entire world";[3] my reading of the Holocaust is that the duty to

---

3. http://talmud.faithweb.com/articles/schindler.html.

act must be imposed by law, not by scripture or ethical codes. A legal obligation to act, and commensurate penalty for failing to act, in the face of potential harm to a total stranger is a powerful lesson taught by the Holocaust.

While in some cases, neighbors observed harm befall neighbors and acquaintances saw acquaintances face danger, the ghettoization, murder, and deportation of European Jewry was watched by people who did not know the victims. Regardless of any possible preexisting relationship between bystander and victim, the consequences are, ultimately, the same for the victim.

Application

Assessing bystander complicity is dependent on the five factors mentioned above—physical proximity to the victim, clarity of the situation, capability of providing assistance, degree of assistance required, and degree of risk intervention implies.

Application of these five criteria ensures criminal prosecution of the bystander will reflect balancing distinct interests and priorities. The discussion is predicated on an assumption that nonintervention is a crime; the question is how and when to move forward with a criminal case.

David Cash

We step away from the Holocaust. We do so using a horrific contemporary example of the bystander. The word "horrific" is used deliberately. For some, the word is an understatement given the facts described below.

The facts are as follows: On May 25, 1997, Jeremy Strohmeyer sexually assaulted and murdered 7-year-old Sherrice Iverson. The murder was committed in the bathroom at the Primadonna Resort and Casino in Primm, Nevada. Strohmeyer, who was convicted and sentenced to life imprisonment, was 19 years old.

David Cash, Jr., Strohmeyer's best friend, observed the assault from the adjacent bathroom stall. Cash made no effort to intervene. When

Strohmeyer confessed to Cash he had just killed Iverson, Cash's only question was whether she had been sexually aroused.

In a newspaper interview, Cash was remarkably defiant: I am not going "to lose sleep over somebody else's problems."[4] In a radio interview Cash said: "I have done nothing wrong."[5] Unfortunately, according to the law, he is correct. It was for that reason the prosecuting attorney was relegated to stating, "Cash will be tried in the court of public opinion."[6]

I have watched Ed Bradley's interview with Cash on *60 Minutes* a number of times. It is beyond disturbing. Whether Cash is a sociopath or a psychopath is beyond my expertise. Today, Cash is gainfully employed with a college degree from the University of California, Berkeley.[7]

Cash is compelling proof of the need for creating legislation imposing legal liability on the bystander. He had the capability to act, was in immediate physical proximity of the victim who was in clear distress and danger, and yet, chose to walk away.

Why?

Because, according to Cash, he "didn't want to stick around and see what was going to materialize."[8]

The moral revulsion arising from Cash's nonintervention, stunning callousness, and deliberate decision to walk away from Sherrice Iverson defies description. Cash was as complicit as a bystander can be when the perpetrator is committing an unimaginable crime.

Victim distress was obvious. The physical distance separating the three could not have been closer.

He is the classic bystander, devoid of any social or moral code of conscience and humanity. In the perfect universe, Cash would have joined Strohmeyer in jail. Unfortunately, he did not. That more than anything highlights the glaring weakness in failing to define the bystander as a criminal—not from the moral perspective but from the legal perspective.

---

4. http://content.time.com/time/magazine/article/0,9171,139892,00.html.

5. Ibid.

6. https://www.youtube.com/watch?v=KqTdXOQmXrc; it is highly recommended the reader watch this deeply troubling segment.

7. http://www.ripoffreport.com/r/David-Cash-Jr-Murder-Accomplice-Works-at-Plains-Exploration-Production-Company-Cash1220/Houston-Texas-77002/David-Cash-Jr-Murder-Accomplice-Works-at-Plains-Exploration-Production-Company-Cash122-575368.

8. http://articles.latimes.com/1998/oct/02/news/ls-28380.

David Cash simply chose not to act. The situation—and its consequences—was clear to him. There is no "gray zone" regarding knowledge,
clarity, capability, and victim distress.

Strohmeyer was sexually assaulting Sherrice. Cash fully understood
that. Sherrice was struggling; Strohmeyer had an arm on her mouth,
muffling her screams. Cash saw that.

Strohmeyer was a 19-year-old male; Sherrice was a 7-year-old girl. The
inherent physical differences, the overwhelming differences in strength
were obviously clear to Cash. And yet, Cash chose to do nothing.

His subsequent comments are outrageous, and his actions are beyond
despicable. The prosecuting attorney's comments regarding the "court of
public opinion" are true. They are also deeply disturbing because they
reflect the lack of consequences. Cash was able to continue with his life
unencumbered.

The interviews suggest a shocking lack of introspection, reflection, and
recognition regarding his decision and its consequences. More importantly, his comments graphically demonstrate how bystanders rationalize
their nonintervention.

That insight is particularly instructive in analyzing the five require-
ments for determining the bystander's criminal responsibility.

Physical Proximity to the Victim

The bystander's physical proximity to the victim is essential for imposing
liability for nonintervention. Regardless of the cause of victim vulnerability, the bystander's obligation to intervene is triggered by *physical
proximity* to the scene of the harm where the victim is vulnerable. The
physical proximity establishes a relationship between bystander and
victim.

The relationship is based on the physical proximity between the two
parties. While the victim's harm or potential harm is the direct result
of perpetrator conduct, the latter is outside the intervention model I
propose.

That is not to free the perpetrator of liability; rather the intention is
to impose liability on the bystander for nonintervention on behalf of the

victim. To do so requires that the bystander be in physical proximity to the victim.

This is in direct contrast to preexisting relationships where physical proximity is irrelevant to the imposition of "duty-to-act" obligations.

The distinction between the two paradigms is critical.

In the bystander-victim relationship at the core of this book, the two individuals have not met previously. They are strangers one to the other. However, in the victim's hour of need, a duty is imposed on the bystander to intervene. When my father and his fellow prisoners were marching through Yugoslavian villages, the bystanders had no previous relationship with them.

Nevertheless, they clearly saw them. Some offered assistance; others taunted or turned a cold shoulder. The fact my father was freed does not excuse the nonintervening villager. There was, clearly, physical proximity between the two; the offer-retraction of water establishes villagers were fully cognizant of the distress of those being forced to march.

Their failure to provide assistance is the essence of complicity. That complicity is—from a liability perspective—predicated on physical proximity.

Physicality is exceptionally important—who is standing where; who sees what; what is the exact distance that separates bystander from victim; how many other individuals, perpetrators, bystanders, and victims are present; what is the time of day; and what are extenuating circumstances, including social, political, and historical.

These are important considerations. However, they do not mitigate, barring exceptional circumstances, the intervention obligation. A bystander's physical proximity enables recognizing victim distress. That is essential to imposing liability on the bystander for nonintervention.

The closer the bystander is to the victim, the greater the opportunity to intervene on behalf of a vulnerable individual. Failure to do so is the essence of complicity. However, intervention need not require actual physical involvement.

Modern methods of communication enable intervention—conveying accurate information, whether to law enforcement or others—regarding victim vulnerability.

Clarity of the Situation

Assessing a situation while it is "ongoing" poses significant challenges to bystanders. Things are not always what they seem to be.

Perhaps the presumed perpetrator is engaged in legitimate self-defense in response to an action initiated by the "victim." Maybe the "victim" has previously engaged in endless verbal bullying of the "perpetrator" who decided, "enough is enough."

The "what-ifs" are endless. They can, doubtlessly, cast significant doubt regarding the true nature of a particular event. Innumerable stories abound highlighting the uncertainty. There is, then, great importance in discerning the facts and circumstances.

Unfortunately, time may be a critical factor; victim vulnerability may be such that the need to intervene is immediate. This poses a burden—or not—on the bystander. The burden is that attempting to understand what is unfolding can be complex; it is not a burden should the bystander decide "uncertainty wins," thereby justifying turning a blind eye to a complex situation. This is the easy way out. It is also a rationalization for failing to recognize victim distress and the compelling need to intervene.

In the event of uncertainty, doubt seeps into the bystander's mind: "Am I seeing what I think I am seeing?" is a reasonable inquiry. In all likelihood it is a question many of us have asked in similar instances. It reflects prudence and caution. On some level, it is also akin to "hedging your bet."

The question is whether it excuses intervention.

The easy answer is "yes, it does"; however, such an approach minimizes the intervention obligation. It creates wiggle room and nuance where both are unwarranted.

Choosing to turn a blind eye, determining that uncertainty outweighs certainty results in harm. More than that, weighing and deliberating and then choosing not to act reflects a conscious decision not to intervene. That is the essence of complicity.

However, there is little doubt that some situations are clearly murky, shrouded in amorphousness. That said, the overwhelming majority of interactions between perpetrator and victim are clear regarding the identity of aggressor and the vulnerable. To accentuate the uncertain is to choose the comfortable. That is not "cost free," as the "comfortable" exacerbates the victim's vulnerability.

Does that explicitly impose criminal liability? Admittedly, this is the gray zone regarding the intervention requirement.

Examples facilitate the discussion.

Bystander Capability

Capability is measured by what action the bystander must undertake to avoid liability and harm. It reflects providing assistance to the victim while minimizing harm to the bystander. There is no intention to unduly endanger the bystander; there is, clearly, desire to impose liability for complicity. Intervention eliminates complicity.

Bystander capability—given the criminal liability for nonintervention—must correspondingly demand minimal effort. The intention is not to create a nonworkable proposal. That is self-defeating. However, there is clear intention to impose a duty to act on the bystander. That is the essence of the balancing approach.

As intervention is the essence of the proposal, the bystander must act. Otherwise, the bystander is complicit in victim harm. That is the primary lesson from the Holocaust: My family's travails are sufficient proof of the profound cost of bystander complicity.

To fully understand this point, we need to return to Nyíregyháza and my grandparents' deportation process.

Tim Cole carefully examines the process of ghettoization and deportation in Hungary. I found his book particularly insightful regarding complicity. Cole details the actions of Hungary's Christian population in transporting Jews from their homes to ghettos.

Through Cole's book I was able to gain—for the first time—insight into the final weeks of my grandparents' lives. I developed much greater appreciation for how bystander complicity contributed to my grandparents' murder in Auschwitz.

The failure to articulate concern, dismay, and opposition to ghettoization; the clear unwillingness to impede the ghettoization process of Nyíregyháza's Jews; the observing as Jews walked or were transported to the train station; and standing akimbo as Jews boarded trains whose destination was Auschwitz are manifestations of bystander complicity.

What were the capabilities of their neighbors as they walked to the train station?

Whether they walked or were transported is, actually, of little significance. What is important, for our purposes, are the actions or nonactions of the bystanders.

In the contemporary age of readily accessible and widely used smartphones, the bystander in physical proximity to the victim, who has assessed the situation at hand, can communicate directly with law enforcement, first responders, or other public service officials.

This is the minimal requirement regarding bystander capability: Utilize modern technology to alert relevant authorities regarding victim vulnerability. The communication need not be elaborate; providing basic information including physical location, number of individuals involved, and need for help is sufficient.

The act of communicating with others requires minimum capability and imposes the least risk on the bystander. This does not demand physical engagement with the victim or perpetrator. It does not impose on the bystander obligation to do more than call attention to a situation of vulnerability and danger. The capability required is minimal.

Are there circumstances where greater involvement and capability would benefit the victim? Needless to say, the answer is yes. Examples throughout history suggest there are individuals who do more than call for help. For that, they are to be lauded and congratulated.

That, however, does not answer the question regarding the Hungarian bystander who observed my grandparents. The means available today, particularly technology, were nonexistent in rural Hungary in May 1944.

The capability discussion, then, must focus on courses of action available to the bystander watching my grandparents. What was he or she capable of doing? What means did they have to intervene? Was it possible to intervene?

The Hungarian bystander did not have a "natural allegiance" to the German occupiers; the Final Solution was not a Hungarian plan. There is no indication that prior to the Second World War Hungarian leadership intended to exterminate its Jewish population. That is also correct regarding the population.

While not gainsaying Hungarian Jewry experienced anti-Semitism, events of post March 1944 were not internally dictated but rather externally imposed. The extraordinary speed with which Hungarian Jewry was deported is compelling proof both of German efficiency and Hungarian complicity.

The complicity was, however, in response to German initiative. The deportation process required significant Hungarian involvement and cooperation. However, in the same vein that the rural population actively participated in the deportation of their Jewish neighbors, they could have chosen to provide solace.

Obviously, they chose not to, but that is not to say they did not have the capability to do so.

Degree of Assistance Required

The question is what level of assistance does the victim require in order to minimize or mitigate the impending harm? The demand is to "do something" alleviating victim vulnerability.

I was confronted with this dilemma three decades ago. I was with a friend when we saw a large crowd gathered around a woman lying on the ground. A closer look made it clear she was having a grand mal epileptic seizure. Those watching her were upset but took no constructive measures to alleviate the situation.

A couple of summers prior to this evening, I had worked in an emergency room and therefore had basic first aid skills. I knew enough to provide the woman assistance until professional first responders arrived.

I believe I did the right thing.

My "hands-on" intervention did not endanger the woman who was clearly in distress. There was, from my perspective, no alternative but to directly intervene. The only criticism that could have been leveled at me was whether I further endangered the woman.

However, because I had the requisite, basic skills I decided to act. My decision to do so was in response to the lack of assistance others were willing to provide.

Perhaps, in retrospect, that compelled me to act.

What should those in the crowd have done? Although cell phones were unavailable, there were restaurants and other establishments in the immediate area. Someone could have, easily, made his or her way to such a place and called for help. They chose not to.

Individually and collectively, people in the crowd failed the young woman. I have long reflected on that evening. What caused a large number of individuals, on a warm, summer evening in a major American city, *not to* provide assistance when doing so would not endanger them? No one would have been harmed should they have stepped forward. This was a "no risk to bystander" situation.

Those in the crowd undoubtedly recognized the need to "do something"; unfortunately, none did. Does that make them liable in the context of my proposal? Are they complicit should harm befall her? None of the bystanders meet what I call the "Cash test" whereby the failure to intervene must be defined as a criminal act.

There was no risk for Cash to intervene; he was not in harm's way. His stated reasons for failing to intervene revolve around not wanting to bother Strohmeyer; worse, in his own words, he had no reason to help Sherrice.

Cash's nonintervention is beyond callous and unforgivable. His conscious decision not to intervene on behalf of Sherrice Iverson should have led to conviction and incarceration.

Acting or Not Acting?

The crowd watching the young woman saw the same thing I did—someone in terrible physical distress. They clearly wanted to do something; yet, they chose not to. No harm would come to them if they chose to provide her assistance; the failure to intervene ensured her continuing harm. That was clear to anyone standing and watching.

The failure to intervene that night was not predicated on malice, evil, or hatred. I do not believe it reflected indifference or apathy. I do not think fear of retribution weighed on people's minds.

I am confident of this because when I began attending to the young woman I immediately asked for warm clothing to cover her. As is the case with grand mal seizure, she was shivering and sweating. The response to my request was immediate.

Men and women alike responded by giving me their sweaters and sport coats. Some placed their clothes directly on me while I was trying to hold her tongue. No one jeered me or hindered my efforts.

None of these people were equivalent to Cash, to the villagers observing my father's Death March, or neighbors watching my grandparents marching to the train station. This is a very different category of bystanders. They were concerned, yet passive, watching yet not responding. There was no evil, but there was no intervention.

In reality, the degree of assistance required was minimal: Run to the nearest place with a phone and call for help. None did so. Yet, the response when I requested assistance was immediate and most helpful. These bystanders were distinct from Cash and Hungarian Gentiles; however, the result could have been the same.

There was, frankly, no justification for nonintervention that night. Victim vulnerability was overwhelming, there was no risk to the intervening bystander, and the degree of assistance required was basic.

Make a damn phone call. Therefore, those in immediate proximity would be liable for failure to intervene according to my minimal intervention model.

Do something. Not doing so may well result in tragedy for which the bystander bears liability.

— 7 —

Duty Owed Is a Legal Obligation— The Bystander's Legal Obligation

Dinner with Friends

At dinner with friends in Salt Lake City, Utah, I was asked to explain my theory. The audience included two attorneys. Both were very skeptical and raised practical concerns focusing on the potential harm to the intervening bystander. One shared that a neighbor was suspected of harming his wife; the other shared a troublesome neighbor was considered "off" by others.

Although the Holocaust represents the most acute—actually, perverse—manifestation of the bystander, it is the garden-variety bystander dilemma that demands resolution.

Both examples reflect bystander dilemmas of everyday life, ones we regularly confront on a daily basis. Should I act? Should I not act? Consider these dilemmas not in the context of a Holocaust but with respect to my neighbor *who needs my help*. The emphasis is on *my help* because the proposed model imposes an obligation regardless of a preexisting relationship.

Simply put: It is immaterial whether I, the bystander, know the person in distress. The critical question is whether there is a vulnerable victim. If yes, then the bystander *must* act. That is the legal obligation that must be imposed on the bystander who would bear the consequences for failing to act.

In both cases my friends suggested intervention must be framed exclusively through the lens of morality. For them, intervention is best perceived as a noble gesture, whereas imposing a legal duty to intervene is, in equal parts, unreasonable and unfeasible.

One has read earlier drafts of this book; his skepticism has been consistent and in his criticisms has referenced other skeptical readers. The other was a "first-time" listener. Both are highly successful, deeply versed in the law, and very thoughtful regarding contemporary events.

I have broken bread with them over the years discussing politics, world events, and everything in between. With one I have shared details of my parents' Holocaust experiences; with the second, that has never been a topic of conversation.

There was no disagreement regarding the horrors of the Holocaust. The point of division was bystander obligation. I have the greatest respect for both and had an inkling that, best efforts aside, my arguments would fall on deaf ears.

Right I was.

In the aftermath of our conversation I have asked myself: Why is it so difficult to convince others regarding the bystander obligation? What is it that others find so unacceptable about imposing an obligation on an individual to assist another individual? The thought of "A" providing assistance to "B" when the former is able and the latter vulnerable strikes me as obvious.

My dinner companions doubtlessly concur. Where we profoundly disagree is whether the assistance be based on "doing the right thing" or a legal obligation. I understand their reliance on the "right thing" argument; however, my analysis of history conclusively demonstrates it represents false hope. I do not know what, if any, hope my grandparents had as they walked to the Nyíergyháza train station that fateful day in May 1944. Whether they believed someone would come to their rescue or not is purely a matter of conjecture.

My instinct suggests they, rightly, had none. It is requested the reader keep this in mind when considering the contemporary examples below. That is not for the purpose of comparing their fate to these incidents, rather the intention is to call the reader's attention to the cost to the victim relying on the bystander "doing the right thing" model.

This is relevant to understanding the underpinning of the proposal, which is to ensure, as much as possible, that the vulnerable victim is offered assistance. The only way that assistance can be guaranteed is by imposing legal obligation on the bystander to act. That is the point of departure for my dinner companions.

Shortly after this dinner, I traveled to a conference in Switzerland unrelated to this book. Nevertheless, the question of bystander responsibility-obligation weighed heavily on my mind, particularly regarding how to more effectively frame the legal obligation argument.

The confluence between the dinner and Switzerland was intellectually interesting because the bystander, individual and institutional, is integral to both. Switzerland represents the institutional bystander that deliberately chose to close its borders, denying refuge to those whose straits can only be described as desperate.

Swiss neutrality, implemented since 1515, defined the country's conduct during the Second World War. Although German and French Jews who entered Switzerland before September 1939 were not deported, Jews seeking haven during the war were denied entry.[1] Switzerland could not have saved all of European Jewry. Nevertheless, the conscious decision to close its borders, in accordance with its historical policy of neutrality, undoubtedly contributed to harm that befell victims of the Final Solution.

The relevance of Swiss neutrality to our inquiry is that the decision to deny entry during the war is akin to the individual bystander refusing to provide assistance to the vulnerable victim. The refusal is a conscious decision, whether by a country or an individual, in the face of harm to an individual.

The legal obligation is, naturally, premised on bystander knowledge. Imposing criminal liability on a bystander who did not know of a particular victim's vulnerability is untenable. As the two examples below

---

1. The policy rationale and an examination of Swiss political history is beyond the scope of this book.

highlight, the knowledge question is essential to assigning liability, and determining bystander knowledge is an evidentiary question.

Whether that conscious decision should be adjudicated by standards of morality or by legal obligation was the point of disagreement at dinner. My two friends focused on the potential harm to an intervening bystander. In doing so, they emphasized my proposal would endanger the bystander with standards of intervention unclear.

Furthermore, they were concerned about on whom the duty can be imposed. That is, can a legal duty be imposed on a bystander merely passing by? Can a duty be imposed on someone standing across the street? Can a duty be imposed on someone in his or her home who hears the neighbors loudly arguing and then hears moving furniture accompanied by yelling and screaming?

Although they reject the proposal, their questions go to the heart of the proposal and its implementability. Our point of departure is their rejection regarding imposition of legal responsibility regardless of the minimal burden I recommend imposing on the bystander.

For them, requiring the bystander alert first responders to an incident is an unviable and untenable obligation. Should the bystander *choose* to do so, that would reflect individual free will, not imposed by society. In that case, the individual would be acting in accordance with his or her particular social and moral code.

The term *upstander*[2] would designate the individual who did the "right thing" as opposed to someone who passively ignores or actively walks away.

Bicycle Accident in Amsterdam and Bystander Nuance

While jogging in Amsterdam (May 2016), I came upon the following scene: A young woman in significant pain following a bicycle accident. I arrived in the immediate aftermath of the accident. The exact

---

2. For a lecture on *Upstander*, see Martha Minow, *Upstanders, Whistle Blowers and Rescuers*, Koningsberger Lecture delivered on December 13, 2014, Utrecht University, the Netherlands.

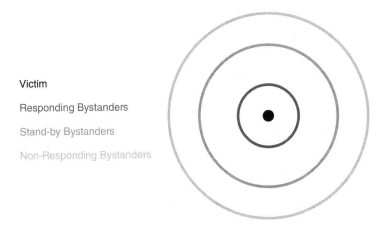

Victim

Responding Bystanders

Stand-by Bystanders

Non-Responding Bystanders

circumstances were unclear to me, but what was striking was the number of people helping her. Some sought to comfort her, another called for emergency help, many were solicitious as to her well-being. My modest contribution was bringing water from a nearby hotel.

The accident occurred on a busy Amsterdam street, about a mile from the Central Train Station, not far from Dam Square. The response of bystanders, the location of the accident, and the question of complicity were of paramount interest to me.

Even though I do not speak Dutch, I was greatly impressed both by the number of passersby who stopped to help and their obvious, genuine concern for her. I assume bicycle accidents are not uncommon in the Netherlands; the sheer number of bicycles can be overwhelming, if not disconcerting. That is important because the scene was—safe to assume—something those responding to her cries had either previously witnessed or personally experienced.

The notion of shared experience, of commonality, is of particular importance. It suggests the familiar, the sense of "this could be me." Meaning, perhaps, the young woman's accident is an event members of Dutch society can readily, perhaps painfully, identify with.[3]

---

3. It was not the first time I have seen a bicycle accident in the 10 years I have regularly been visiting the Netherlands. Like many other visitors, I, too, have been on the wrong end of a bicycle rider surprised by my lack of understanding that bicycles have the absolute right of way. I am, in the Netherlands, more wary of bicycles than cars.

Obviously the circumstances are different, but upon closer examination they warrant deeper analysis.

From the interaction between the injured bicyclist and her assisters, the following were quickly apparent: They did not know her, Dutch was the common language, and she was engaged in an activity integral to the Dutch way of life. That is, they shared deep bonds and similarities. Commonality is, I believe, an essential element in an instinctive decision to render assistance to another. The word *another* is deliberately used to distinguish from the *other*.

"Other" described Jews during the Holocaust; the word connotates outsider, clearly not one of "us." That is, I suggest, distinct from "another"; that term suggests a fellow member of society with whom there is a natural affinity and commonality. The distinction is, seemingly, important in the bystander discussion: It is more natural to come to the assistance of someone I can relate to than of someone who is not like me.

The woman riding her bike on a main thoroughfare in Amsterdam was engaged in an activity all members of Dutch society can relate to. The cliché that the Dutch are born with a bicycle is oft-heard. However, in dramatic contrast, Jews walking to the train platform, carrying their belongings, under armed guard present a very different dilemma. The natural affinity, immediate understanding of her need for help, are not instinctively present when observing the Jews.

As to the similarities, both the bicyclist and deported Jews were in distress in full view of the public, on busy streets in a major town. Her plight was obvious; the Jews walking to Amsterdam's Central Train Station, carrying their bags while, largely, formally attired,[4] were also in great plight. However, one victim category elicited an immediate, positive response, whereas the other, largely, did not.

The two situations are essential to understanding the bystander dilemma. Obviously, the visuals relevant to the two situations are distinctly different. Nevertheless, there are important similarities,

---

4. Pictures of Jews walking to train stations depict men dressed in suits or coats and ties, women wearing dresses, and children nicely dressed, and all age appropriate. For me, that is one of the most striking visuals of the deportation process.

particularly the image of something amiss. The woman on the ground was in clear pain, needing immediate assistance.

If those walking on the sidewalk stepped around the young woman—either looked or did not—it was impossible to ignore her cries of pain—and continued on their journey, they would enhance her predicament. She was lying on her side, grabbing her leg, and calling for help.

Jews making their way on the same street to the Central Train Station had been removed from their homes, given little time to gather their belongings, and ordered to immediately leave the world they knew.

Neither justifies the bystander watching and not providing assistance. In both cases, not providing assistance compounds harm and danger. Fortunately, passersby heeded her call and provided much needed assistance. To do otherwise would endanger the vulnerable victim; that is what the criminal bystander does. It is the essence of the *failure* of the greater Dutch population decades ago.

I use the word *failure* with mixed feelings: Dutch friends are invariably quick to point out the courage of their relatives under extremely difficult circumstances. I have the greatest respect for their actions, but I am unable to ignore the remarkably high rate of Dutch Jews who were deported.

The juxtaposition between historical Dutch tolerance, devoid of anti-Semitism that plagued other European countries, and Dutch accommodation and efficiency in collaborating with the Nazis has weighed heavily on my mind over the years. It is, for me, a *non sequitor*. Nevertheless, it is the reality that characterizes the years 1940–1945.[5]

An enlightening conversation with a seatmate on a KLM flight to Amsterdam from Salt Lake City, Utah, shed interesting light on this seeming paradox. My seatmate was a retired seventy-two-year-old Dutch pharmacist living in the city of Utrecht, the Netherlands.

By chance, I have spent significant time in Utrecht over the years: I wrote much of my previous book, *Freedom from Religion*, while

---

5. I was saddened to learn from a Dutch friend that there are sharp cut-backs in the teaching of history in schools.

teaching at Utrecht University. A small statue honoring Anne Frank that I passed every morning from my bed and breakfast to my office greatly moved me. That daily walk led me, in part, to dedicate the book to Anne Frank.

That background was on my mind when my seatmate inquired as to my travels and work. Although I generally seek to avoid interaction with those sitting next to me on flights, a couple of conversations over the years have provided me important material for books. In this case, I decided to share this project with the gentleman, including my years-long inability to reconcile the rate of deportation of Dutch Jewry.

His response was one I had not previously heard: Calvinism is at the heart of Dutch obedience to authority, regardless what or who the authority figure is. In many previous conversations the terms suggested to me—albeit not exclusively—to explain the extraordinarily high rate of deportation were "efficiency" as a cultural trait, flat topography suggesting difficulty in using terrain for hiding purposes, and that "Dutch society was heavily pillarized before the war."[6]

My seatmate was skeptical regarding my suggestion that "accommodation," either with or to authority, explains the number of deported Jews. For him, the concept, philosophically and practically, of obedience to authority was essential to understanding Dutch action or inaction regarding deportation of Jews.

When I explained to him my, for lack of a better term, obsession with the concept of complicity, his response was quick: Obedience is the essence of complicity. He did not, I am convinced, intend to suggest "obedience" as an excuse but rather as an explanation. There is a sharp difference between the two. Whether Dutch action is understood to be predicated on *obedience, accommodation, efficiency,* or a combination of the three, the end result is the same.

All three, individually and collectively, suggest complicity, whose consequences are a matter of historical record. Regardless of the motivation—individual, cultural, or societal—complicity is essential to understanding the bystander.

---

6. Email sent to me; in my private records.

Bystander Silence

However, bystander silence can also be a positive from the victim's perspective.

Case in point: On May 15, 2016, I met with a Holocaust survivor, A.[7] In the course of our two-hour conversation, A shared with me a number of facts regarding her childhood, how she was hidden-saved, and the circumstances of her experiences. One issue is of particular importance to us: While in hiding she continued going to school on a daily basis. Neighbors clearly observed a small child who they knew was not the daughter of the courageous woman who hid A. Yet they chose not to report this to the authorities.

In the aftermath of our meeting, I wondered how to describe-define the nonreporting neighbors. According to A they were not heroes— a term she very specifically and deliberately applied only to the woman who hid her. The neighbors were passive in that they did not inform—in direct contrast to the neighbor(s) who on two separate occasions "ratted" my mother to the Hungarian authorities.

However, both—the neighbors who did not report and the neighbors who did report—made a conscious decision to act. Although in A's case the action was a "nonaction" and in my mother's case the action was an "action," both reflect a decision made. Both were bystanders in that they were not directly involved.

Unlike in A's case, my mother's neighbors morphed from bystander to perpetrator; their decision to inform the authorities regarding my mother's and grandmother's hiding place reflects active collaboration. That act of complicity goes significantly beyond the nonintervening bystander who observed my father on his Death March through Yugoslavian villages. That is not to free the villager from complicity; it is, however, intended to illuminate the nuance regarding the bystander and complicity.

The neighbors who did not "out" A were passive, as were the villagers who chose not to provide assistance to my father. However, their passivity must not be viewed as reflective of "nonaction," for both acted by not acting. That nonaction in A's case was a positive, whereas in my father's case it had negative repercussions for it heightened the danger to which he was exposed.

---

7. The records of the meeting are in my private notes.

The word *passivity* suggests not doing anything. It is used to describe an individual not engaged, lethargic, and indifferent to events, whether in his immediate environs or elsewhere. It is a quality I find unfathomable; I am hard pressed to identify anyone in my social circle who is passive.

The thought of resignation as a motif of the human condition—whether existential or practical—lends itself to political regimes that endanger the public, facilitate discrimination and xenophobia, and oftentimes result in identifying, without basis, the "other" as the common enemy. The suggestion that passivity fosters fascism or Nazism is not without merit.

However, the discussion is not as simple as it seems at first blush. Passivity is not inherently a negative, common assumptions notwithstanding. A's comments make that perfectly clear. That is not the case with my father's experience. Nevertheless, in both instances the bystander chose not to act. That phrasing is appropriate provided the word *act* is defined as a clearly defined physical action such as walking, talking, offering relief, calling for help or some other clearly physical action.

I suggest what is otherwise commonly understood to be "passive" conduct needs to be viewed, *circumstance dependent,* as a positive with important consequences for the endangered individual. In the same vein, that same decision not to act, circumstance dependent, can have tragic consequences for the "at-risk" individual.

The villager could not have predicated, or assumed, Tito's partisan fighters would kill the camp guards leading the Death March, thereby freeing my father and his fellow prisoners. That had certainly not been the case regarding the first group of Jewish prisoners ostensibly released from Bor only to be massacred upon reaching the Hungarian border. I do not know what, if any, actions villagers took on behalf of the first group. That is in contrast to the second group, based on my conversations with my father.

My Neighbor's Child

The victim in the street raises significantly fewer questions than loud noises from the neighbors' house. Admittedly, there is greater uncertainty if the victim—or assumed victim—cannot be seen, as is the case with yelling at the neighbors' house.

This is, without doubt, a situation posing greater uncertainty to the bystander. That is obvious. In addition, unlike the victim in the street situation, the person hearing an argument does not know who else is hearing the same argument.

More than that, the neighbor does not know if anyone else is within hearing range. Both dilemmas, the victim in the street and the yelling at the neighbors, represent everyday challenges and quandaries facing members of society. In both cases, harm may well befall an individual. In both cases, it is unclear if someone will intervene.

In the apartment situation, the unknowns significantly outweigh the knowns. That is the reality; that is the situation dilemma confronting the neighbor who hears the argument, the yelling, and the attendant escalation.

Many of us have been in this situation; some of us have acted by calling the police or by inquiring whether something is amiss. The reality is that most of us choose not to act, shrug our shoulders, and continue with our affairs. This is what I did when a neighbor who lived across the street locked his young child out of the house at night.

The child—a boy aged approximately 8 years old—cried throughout the night. I had had no previous interaction with the parents; I did not know their names or anything about them. To the best of my recollection, we never exchanged basic salutations.

Why did I not act? For the same reasons most of us make the same decision.

Was there a crime? There is no doubt the father committed a crime: It was winter, it was cold, and the child was endangered by the conditions. However, because of my inaction, and that of my fellow neighbors, no action was taken against the father.

There was no rational justification for my failure to alert the police. No danger was foreseeable were I to have simply picked up the phone. The abusive father would never have known who called the police. There is no chance he would have harmed me or my family.

In other words, I was a classic bystander who turned his shoulder to a victim in clear distress. The vulnerability was obvious as the child cried, begging his parents to open the door. At some point I fell asleep; I do not know when the child was allowed back into the house.

Did I commit a crime? Am I liable for failing to alert law enforcement to a clear case of child abuse? According to existing law, no preexisting relationship exists, and I was not the actor who locked the child out of the house. I clearly failed the child morally, but that is not the question before us. According to my dinner companions and others who agree with their analysis of the bystander, I am not guilty of any crime, for no crime exists addressing my nonaction.

This situation, as unpleasant and troubling as it was, is no different from countless others occurring on a daily basis. There is no intent to equate the child's distress to that faced by European Jewry. However, the rationale for my recommendation is based on a primary lesson learned from the Holocaust: *silence and nonaction kill.*

Legislation

For that reason, I believe legislation must be drafted imposing on the bystander the obligation to act. The follow-up question is who is the bystander in this particular situation and do we impose on law enforcement-prosecutors the requirement to interview all neighbors within reasonable earshot with an eye to their indictment? The reader will note this is different from the incident in the street situation where bystanders are more easily identifiable.

Indictment is evidentiary dependent and just as is the case with other crimes, the duty would be imposed on law enforcement to gather evidence to determine who violated the law. A caveat is in order: In recommending legislation be drafted, it is a matter of jurisdictional discretion and authority to determine whether the crime of nonintervention is a misdemeanor or felony and what is the appropriate punishment. Possible punishment includes a citation akin to a traffic violation, a fine, probation, and incarceration.

The reader will recall the model I am proposing imposes minimal intervention—actually nothing more than calling for assistance. The proposal does not require physical intervention, does not impose an undue burden on the bystander, and requires no interaction with the perpetrator. In other words, at minimal cost to the bystander, a vulnerable "at-risk" victim is provided critical assistance.

Two Contemporary Incidents

The two stories below are particularly relevant; I have placed in bold format particular words essential for our purposes.

Glad Someone Called

Around midnight Thursday, deputies went to a house near San Antonio after somebody called to report hearing a child crying in a backyard, according to a Friday news release from the Bexar County Sheriff's Office.

The deputies knocked on the front door, got no answer, and went around back, using a ladder to look over the fence, said James Keith, spokesman for the sheriff's office.

They saw two toddlers in a state that Keith struggled to describe.

A 2-year-old boy was "chained to the ground as if he was a dog," he said. "There was no slack in the chain. His pants were down. You could tell he'd been here for a while. And then a short distance away, a 3-year-old girl who was tied to a door with a dog leash who was just exhausted."

The deputies moved quickly to release the two youngsters, but their work was not finished.

Inside the house, they discovered six children ranging in age from 10 months to 13 years, the release said. There were no adults on site to care for them.

"To describe this as disturbing is an understatement," Keith said. "It makes you wonder what somebody's thinking. How could they do this?"

Early Friday morning, the parents of the six children who were inside returned to the house, the sheriff's office said.

The mother, Porucha Phillips, 34, was believed to be responsible for caring for the two toddlers, authorities said. She was charged with injury to a child by omission with serious bodily injury and injury to a child by omission with bodily injury and is being held in the Bexar County Jail.

Deputies haven't said they're searching for the parents of the toddlers found in the backyard.

The toddlers were taken to the Children's Hospital of San Antonio and are recovering, though the girl is in intensive care, Keith said.

Child Protective Services said one of them has a fractured right arm and wrist and the other has superficial injuries including abrasions and scarring. Six children have been cleared for foster care.

CPS said it had no prior involvement with the family, KSAT said. Authorities are investigating a report that a day care might have been operating out of the home, KSAT reported.

Neighbors and authorities said they were horrified by the conditions the children were found in.

"When we heard of it, it was bad," Christina Rivera, who lives nearby, told KSAT. "It was shocking. Especially something happening across the street and we didn't even know about it or see it."

*Keith said he was **glad somebody thought to call the sheriff's office.***

He encouraged anybody who ever suspects child abuse to do the same.

***"We are grateful that this person was brave enough to call us and that our deputies were able to respond when they did,"** he said to KSAT. "I don't even want to think about how this could have happened, how this could have played out, had our deputies not gotten there when they did."*[8]

---

8. http://www.cnn.com/2016/04/29/us/texas-toddlers-tied-up-in-backyard/index.html.

No One Came

CHICAGO—Police are seeking two suspects in the brutal beating of a woman who was riding the CTA Blue Line yesterday morning.

The beating happened around 10 a.m. Thursday on a CTA Blue Line train headed west, approaching the Kedzie-Homan stop.

Nineteen-year-old DePaul student Jessica Hughes was on her way home to Berwyn from a morning class and says after a large group of people got off the train at the UIC Halstead stop, a man moved to the seat in front of her, turned around and attacked.

"He grabs me, pushes me to the floor and starts beating on my head repeatedly," Jessica said.

The man wanted Jessica's phone. It was in her pocket. A woman who was with the attacker jumped in and punched Jessica in the nose, breaking it.

All the while, two male passengers stood by and watched.

"He kept beating on me. I'm yelling help to the other people and no one came."

The suspects did not get Jessica's phone. They ran off the train.

The attackers were captured on surveillance video.

"I'm just hoping everything they need is on that video," Jessica said. "And they're able to get those people that did this to me."

She described the attacker as an African American man in his mid-20s. She says he had facial hair, was wearing a blue Ralph Lauren polo hat, a grey hoodie and baggy pants that were sagging below his waist.

She says the woman, also African American in her mid-20s, was extremely thin, with long black hair.

Chicago police are investigating, but had not interviewed Jessica yet when WGN News spoke with her earlier this afternoon.[9]

Both stories, troubling and tragic as they are, reflect the everyday instances my proposal targets. In both instances there were bystanders: In the first

---

9. http://wgntv.com/2016/04/29/woman-attacked-while-riding-blue-line-suspects-sought/.

neighbors heard the toddlers, in the second two bystanders saw the beating. The first story is similar to the situation in which I failed to act, the second conjures up images of Kitty Genovese.

Kitty Genovese

It is impossible to write a book about the bystander without referencing arguably the most well-known instance of bystander nonaction. Although some of the original facts have recently been called into question,[10] the following brief re-counting is relevant:

> *A half-century after the slow killing of Ms. Genovese, which began in the dead of night on a deserted street in Kew Gardens, Queens, and ended half an hour later in the vestibule of her building, the case still resonates with terror and collective regret in the popular imagination, sustained by films, books, behavioral studies, psychology classes and endless debates over the responsibilities of citizens who witness a crime. . . .*
>
> *Ghastly as the details of Mr. Moseley's attack were—selecting Ms. Genovese at random, stabbing her at least 14 times as she screamed and pleaded for help, retreating into the shadows as lights went on in apartments overhead, returning to rape and finally kill her—they by themselves might not have placed the case, or the Moseley name, into the annals of crime.*
>
> *Two weeks later,* The Times *published a . . . flawed front-page account quoting the police and Ms. Genovese's neighbors. "For more than half an hour 38 respectable, law-abiding citizens watched a killer stalk and stab a woman in three separate attacks in Kew Gardens," it began.*
>
> *"Twice the sound of their voices and the sudden glow of their bedroom lights interrupted him and frightened him off. Each time he returned, sought her out and stabbed her again. Not one person*

---

10. Kevin Cook, *Kitty Genovese: The Murder, The Bystanders, The Crime That Changed America,* W.W. Norton, New York, 2014.

telephoned the police during the assault; one witness called after the woman was dead."[11]

What Do We Learn?

The phrases I chose to highlight in the stories of the two recent incidents go to the crux of the discussion:

1. Glad somebody thought to call the sheriff's office.
2. He encouraged anybody who ever suspects child abuse to do the same.
3. "We are grateful that this person was brave enough to call us and that our deputies were able to respond when they did."
4. All the while, two male passengers stood by and watched.
5. "He kept beating on me. I'm yelling help to the other people and no one came."

All five phrases reflect the conundrum that demands resolution. The sheriff and victim unintentionally highlight the weakness of the contemporary bystander-victim relationship. As previously noted, the perpetrators—while undoubtedly responsible for heinous crimes—are not integral to our analysis though they are primarily responsible for victim harm. That, however, is beside the point when examining bystander obligation.

Sheriff Keith's comments had, seemingly, two objectives—to congratulate the individual who called the police and to encourage others to do the same if faced with similar facts. My dinner companions would, it is safe to assume, concur with Sheriff Keith. I could not more emphatically disagree. His words highlight the inherent weakness of the existing bystander-victim relationship.

In "encouraging" others to act, he is reinforcing the "right thing" model which, yet again, has left another victim vulnerable. Relying on that

---

11. http://www.nytimes.com/2016/04/05/nyregion/winston-moseley-81-killer-of-kitty-genovese-dies-in-prison.html.

model exposes the vulnerable victim to harm. Imposing a legal liability would—at the least—heighten awareness regarding the obligation to act.

There is no expectation that all neighbors will act; to assume that would be unreasonable. However, knowledge that hiding behind "we did not hear-see-know" carries potential legal action would, undoubtedly, compel a greater number of bystanders to act.

Conviction—citation, misdemeanor, or felony—carries with it negative repercussions and implications. It is something most of us wish to avoid, particularly when the required action imposes minimal obligation.

The sheriff's department received only one phone call, whereas others, according to the report, claimed not to have heard the chained children: "It was shocking. Especially something happening across the street and we didn't even know about it or see it."

The words, uttered by a neighbor, are not convincing, particularly in relation to the fact that somebody called to report hearing a child crying in a backyard.

In other words, the claim of ignorance is unconvincing. It is, however, tolerated and acceptable by the law presently. In the same way, the two men who watched the beating of the train victim could stand, passively, while a man and woman viciously attacked Ms. Hughes. In her statement, Ms. Hughes highlights, much like Sheriff Keith, the inherent and dangerous weakness of the contemporary bystander-victim relationship.

The two men clearly saw the attack; the physicality of the circumstances as Ms. Hughes describes leaves nothing to the imagination. The train was largely empty, two people attacked the victim, and two people watched the attack. The fate of the two perpetrators remains to be seen; the fate of the two bystanders is clear. They will not be arrested or prosecuted. They are free to board another train and continue as if nothing occurred.

The train beating victim comment recalls the tragic murder of Kitty Genovese. As horrific as Genovese's death was, there is something more visceral regarding the bystander in the train beating. The two bystanders were standing right there.

There is no doubt that my conviction regarding bystander obligation is a direct result of my family's tragedies and tribulations. That must be obvious to the reader. Proposing that failure to intervene be a crime is intended to ensure the bystander passivity that was critical to Nazi success does not go unpunished.

This is not intended as retributive, albeit, perhaps, it has that ring. Quite the opposite: The intention is to ensure that future victims whether of calamities or everyday occurrences not be left unprotected in the face of impending harm.

When asked what I have learned from studying the Holocaust, my response is consistent: Where was the bystander and how could neighbors watch neighbors be brutally victimized? My concern is not with beneficiaries who took furniture left behind by deported Jews or entered deserted apartments; that category of perpetrator is of no interest to me.

A thief is a thief, and a trespasser is a trespasser; in both cases, the criminal law accounts for them. These criminals are commonly understood to be liable for their actions; culpability is beyond question for someone who takes the property of another, regardless of the circumstances. The perpetrator, regardless of the severity of actions, is distinguishable from the bystander.

The guilt of the former is a matter for existing criminal codes; the guilt of the latter is, for many, to be viewed through the lens of morality exclusively.

The question is why.

In innumerable conversations, whether with lawyers, friends, family, or others with whom I have interacted while writing this book, the answer to that inquiry revolves around a common theme: *The bystander is not responsible for victim plight* and *imposition of duty to act is unreasonable.* The perpetrator is responsible for victim precariousness.

Simply put, according to this argument, the bystander who acts is a moral hero; the bystander who chose not to act made a reasonable decision.

— 8 —

Maastricht, The Netherlands: Summer 2016

Maastricht

Previously, I referenced my June 2015 trip to Maastricht; that visit served as the backdrop to my decision to spend five days in Maastricht in May–June 2016.

The decision was based on my belief that exploring, in depth, the deportation process in one city through the lens and experience of local townspeople and their descendants would shed powerful light on the dilemma of the bystander. Sharing with the reader specific stories of particular people is intended to facilitate that discussion.

The decision doubtlessly was influenced by my introduction to the Stumbling Stones project Professor Fred Grunfeld has spearheaded.[1]

While visiting the Stumbling Stones exhibit in Maastricht[2] with Professor Grunfeld, we came upon an elderly Dutch woman. Speaking in a combination of Dutch and English I learned of the woman's mother's

---

1. See page 27 for Stumbling Stone at entrance to Professor Grunfeld's home.
2. http://www.struikelsteentjes-maastricht.nl.

bravery. What was interesting was her rejection of my use of the word "heroic"; her siblings referred to the decision as "stupid."

The difference is the following: From my perspective, the mother saved a child; from the woman's perspective, the mother endangered her own children in doing so. The difference is not semantic, rather instructive when considering the bystander, which her mother clearly was not.

The mother, like others who hid Jews, willingly incurred risk and danger. Numbers tell the following story: At the beginning of German occupation of Holland, there were 500 Jews living in Maastricht; of those, approximately 290 were deported, the remainder went into hiding.

Although some hiders were arrested, there is no known report of German soldiers or Dutch police killing hiders. That, obviously, was not known at the time for the assumption was harm would befall hiders. Nevertheless, thousands of individuals and families willingly hid Jews. Maastricht Jews were primarily hidden in Maastricht and nearby Belgian towns on the Dutch-Belgian border, which is minutes away from Maastricht. In addition, Jews from Amsterdam and Rotterdam hid in Maastricht.

August 24, 1942, Summons and August 25, 1942, Deportation

On Monday, August 24, 1942, Maastricht's Jewish population received summons ordering them to report the next day to the school located at Professor Pieter Willemsstraat.[3] The summons informed the Jews they should prepare for hard labor; clear instructions were given regarding what luggage to bring when reporting. The Jewish community before, during, and after the August 1942 deportation is depicted on the next page.

Those who decided to report arrived by foot, were driven by friends or neighbors, or otherwise made their way to the school. One group, who lived on Hoofdstraat, were driven by bus to the school. Upon arrival at the school the Jews were subject to medical examinations. Those deemed

---

3. The summons was issued in accordance with a list of the town's Jews prepared by the Jewish Council.

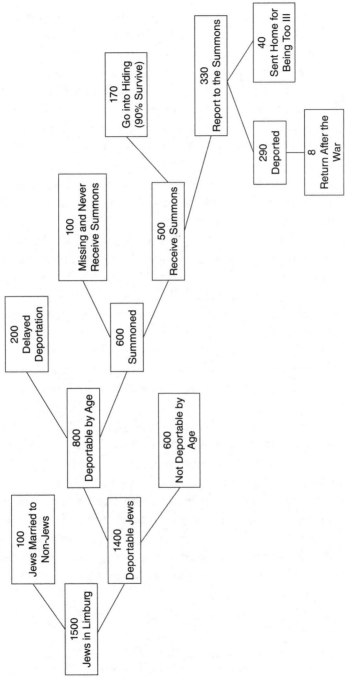

Chart depicting Maastricht deportation statistics

too ill or infirm were sent home. Of the 350 Jews who reported to the school, fifty were sent home after being deemed too ill or infirm.

Deportation from the school to Maastricht's train station—a distance of approximately 300 meters—occurred around midnight August 25, 1942. The apparent reason for the late hour was a calculated desire not to "upset" the local population whom the Germans considered "almost" Aryan. From the train station the Jews were transported to Westerbork Transit Camp.[4] On August 28 they were deported to Auschwitz. The overwhelming majority were murdered upon arrival on August 31.

The three-step process—home to school, school to train station, train station to deportation—was overwhelmingly unimpeded. The local population neither interfered nor intervened on behalf of the Jewish population acting in accordance with the "order to report." This I learned from interviews with individuals who witnessed the deportation in which they emphasized the orderly process in which Jews left their homes, with their luggage, and alighted awaiting vehicles.

As evidenced by an absolute minimum of policemen involved in the deportation process, the authorities did not expect resistance. The lack of both Jewish resistance and public interference-intervention in the face of deportations has been explained as reflecting traditional Dutch obedience to authority and the lack of a military culture in the Netherlands.[5]

That explanation has similarly been proffered regarding the relatively late development of an active Dutch resistance in response to the German occupation. That is distinct from hiders who actively assisted Jews defying deportation orders.

According to C[6] who lived on a street with a significant Jewish population, the deportation to the school was conducted under the watchful eye of a single German neighbor[7] wearing a German military uniform. C shared with me that the evening prior to deportation her father spoke with one of the neighbors, Mr. Salamon. According to C, Mr. Salamon

---

4. https://www.ushmm.org/wlc/en/article.php?ModuleId=10005217.
5. Holland was neutral in the First World War.
6. Records of all meetings are in my notes; all individuals I interviewed are noted either by an initial or initials only. I met C in her home on May 30, 2016.
7. Meaning the neighbor—Mr. Messinger—lived in Holland but was originally from Germany.

told her father orders had been received to report the following day to the school for the purpose of transfer to a labor camp.

Mr. Salamon informed C's father that he planned on going into hiding[8] with his wife and children rather than report as ordered. On the day of the deportation, one bus was to take the Jews from C's street to the school. From our conversation I learned the Jews, while emotional, boarded the bus without posing a burden to the driver or Mr. Messinger who was unarmed, according to C.

Neighbors who watched did not interfere or come to the aid of the Jews. There was a mutual taking of leave one from the other, either verbally or with a wave of the hand.

The same recounting of no resistance offered by the Jews was given by L. Similar to C, L was twelve years old when Maastricht's Jews were deported. In our conversation, he shared with me that he observed many Jews walking in an orderly fashion, escorted by one municipal policeman. L saw a Jewish friend, Mieneke Os, walk with her mother. According to L, he observed the marchers for approximately thirty minutes.

As I have come to learn, the Os family was killed in Auschwitz. In his recounting, L emphasized the Jews seemed resigned to their fate—in Dutch he used the expression "sheep to their slaughter"—walking silently to the school. L did not notice if there were other observers.

When I asked C and L how did their parents respond to the deportation, their answers were remarkably similar: There was a war going on, the Allies were bombing, there was a food shortage, and families had to focus on their own problems and challenges. In other words, while sad about, and for, the Jews, they had their own problems. That is beyond reasonable and totally understandable.

It also raises legitimate queries regarding the bystander and complicity. The question focuses on to whom is a duty owed. While it would be unreasonable, given their respective ages, to impose on C and L an intervention obligation on behalf of the Jews, can that obligation not

---

8. The correct term is "diving," which signifies hiding; there is no connection between "diving" and an underground hiding place, as a diver could be in hiding on a rooftop. Those providing haven were "hiders."

be imposed on their parents? To answer that, we need to more closely examine the conditions and circumstances.

According to L, he did not know in advance of the deportation and it was happenstance that he observed the Jews walking to the school at 11 a.m., August 25, 1942. He reported to his parents that evening what he had witnessed earlier in the day. In other words, by the time his parents knew, according to L, the Jews were already in the school, hours away from boarding the trains taking them to Westerbork. As his parents had not witnessed the walk, there is no rational basis for imposing any duty on the parents.

That, however, is not necessarily the case regarding C's parents. According to C, Mr. Salamon informed her father the previous evening that Maastricht's Jews had received the reporting order and that he intended to "dive" with his family. According to C, her mother was with her when Jews living on their street boarded the bus taking them to the school.

In both cases, neither offered practical assistance to the Jews who lived on their street. Was this lack of positive action in the face of clear and imminent danger akin to complicity? Rearticulated, were C's parents bystanders who could have acted on behalf of their neighbors? It is a question that cannot be answered in full because we do not know if her father offered haven to Mr. Salamon or if he sought out other Jews who lived on his street.

As all involved have passed, we cannot inquire. However, regarding C's mother we know she observed Jews boarding the bus but took no measures on their behalf. We also know from C that the boarding process was overseen by one neighbor wearing a German military uniform.

The question regarding C's mother's complicity is, of course, moot as she, too, has passed. However, were the events to unfold today, the decision whether to prosecute or not would be a "closer call" than regarding C's father.

April 9, 1943: A Bystander's Child, 75 Years Later

My meeting with L.S. was particularly relevant to this question. While L.S. was witness to the deportation of April 9, 1943, the third and last deportation of Maastricht Jewry, her comments regarding the bystander are appropriately included here.

It was, without doubt, a most moving and powerful conversation. We met in her home; she graciously answered my many questions, never flinching from honestly discussing her father. What follows is my recounting of the meeting sent to a friend shortly after it ended:

As her English isn't very good, there was a translator:

When she was 11 years old, she was told to say goodbye to her Jewish neighbors, the Waynkowski family, who had a 13-year-old boy (her friend), a 4-year-old daughter and the mother (it is unclear where the father was . . . records aren't clear on this point).

She lived with her father and 6 siblings (her mother had previously died).

On THE day (April 9, 1943) she crossed the street with her sister to say goodbye.

The 13-year-old had previously given her his book collection for safekeeping.

When they went to say goodbye her sister was given the 4-year-old's doll (she doesn't remember if the mom or girl gave it) for safekeeping.

After saying goodbye they went home.

She stood inside their house with her father watching the family board the truck that took them away.

She said it was first time she ever saw her father cry.

She said those who stood and did nothing had "no guts" . . . she then corrected herself and said "they were cowards" . . . there was LONGGGGG pause . . . with tears in her eyes she said "I guess my father was a coward."

She then added "maybe he didn't act because he had 7 children and no wife." But then repeated that "yes, maybe he was a coward."

In retrospect, she feels non-Jews should-could have done more to save the Jews and sees her own father as perfect example.

We met for over an hour, speaking quietly.

Was pretty overwhelming.

Marcelle Devries—Background and Deportation

The reader will recall Professor Grunfeld insisted I carefully examine the Stumbling Stone before entering his home last summer. It was after learning the story of Marcelle Devries, her family, her fate, and the family home, did I decide to undertake the week-long trip to Maastricht. I did so because of my conviction that focusing on an individual would compellingly place the bystander-victim discussion under the bright lights.

To do this required focusing on the particular circumstances of her deportation, both specific to Marcelle and in the broader context of life in Maastricht. Those with whom I met helped me understand the conditions and circumstances of both the August 1942 deportation and the relations between Jew and Gentile in Maastricht.

When Marcelle received the summons on Monday, August 25, 1942, she was 36 years old, living at home with her parents. Marcelle was not married. Neither of her siblings, a brother and sister, lived in Maastricht. Her parents owned a factory located in the back of the large and spacious family house.[9]

The Devries were the only Jewish family in their immediate neighborhood; this was not unusual in Maastricht given the relative smallness of the Jewish community. The only exception was Hoofdstraat where a number of Jewish families lived.

The words *polite*, *cordial*, and *correct* were used to explain Jewish-Gentile relations. Anti-Semitism was not an issue in Maastricht—Jews were members of a larger society and a Jewish-religious culture was limited. Assimilation meant Jews were not "openly Jewish" as tolerance was premised on the minority's accommodation to the majority's culture.

Jews who could practice their faith in the privacy of their homes but not publicly primarily earned their living as butchers, peddlers, and sellers of scrap iron. The term *marginal occupations* was suggested.

Dutch society was "pillarized" into four main pillars: Catholics, Protestants, Socialists, and liberals. Jews were primarily, but not exclusively, allied with the Socialist pillar as some belonged to the liberal pillar. In

---

9. The house is currently owned by Professor Grunfeld.

Maastricht, there was one synagogue. The province of Limburg, of which Maastricht is the largest city, is overwhelmingly Catholic.

The summons arrived during the day, August 24, 1942. We do not know if Marcelle or her parents had prior knowledge, as was the case with Mr. Salamon, of the summons. She worked in an administrative position in Maastricht; the one picture I have seen of Marcelle depicts a woman in her thirties in a male working environment.

She did not work in the family business but was, clearly, devoted to her parents. It was suggested she was the sibling whose role was to take care of her parents: Mr. Devries was sixty-two when Marcelle was deported, Mrs. Devries was in her late fifties. Some have offered that Marcelle reported as ordered in order to "spare her parents."

The parents went into hiding as did her sister; her brother escaped to Switzerland with his wife where he had one child, born in 1944. Marcelle's sister married after the war. In other words, Marcelle was the sole family member murdered in the Holocaust.

On Tuesday, August 25, 1942, Marcelle took leave of her parents. We know that a neighbor, Mr. Eurling, took her to the school in horse and carriage.

On June 2, 2016, Professor Grunfeld and I met with ME, Mr. Eurling's daughter. The meeting, not planned in advance, was held in the village of Smeermaes near the Dutch-Belgian border.

I requested the meeting as it was particularly important for me to gain insight into what Marcelle understood, what she believed, and what she recognized regarding the nature of the summons and the fate that awaited her. This is of great importance regarding victim knowledge and expectation; this is a crucial linchpin in the victim-bystander relationship.

I wanted to know what they spoke about, if anything, on the five- to ten-minute car ride from the house to the school. After all, Mr. Eurling is the last known individual with whom she spoke; that is not to suggest she did not speak with others prior to her murder, but the neighbor is the last one whose identity is known.

Similarly, I was hoping the daughter would shed light on any comments her father made upon his return home regarding whether other Maastricht residents were in the streets, observing Jews walking to the school. I was curious whether the father suggested to either his daughter or his wife that he had offered to protect—hide—Marcelle and if yes, what her response to such an offer had been.

I was curious what an adult—Mr. Eurling—might have shared with his family upon returning home: Did he slap himself on the forehead and say "what have you done"? or, perhaps, did the family disregard the plight of the Jews?

It was suggested Mr. Eurling offered to take Marcelle because of the heavy suitcase she was to carry to the school. Others, however, walked from different distances; nevertheless, Marcelle was taken. We do not know if Mr. Devries initiated the request, or if Mr. Eurling observed her at the beginning of the walk and quickly offered her a ride; we do not know if Marcelle approached him prior to leaving the house.

In our meeting with ME, we learned the following:

ME, who was 10 years old in August 1942, does not recall if the Devries stood outside their home waving good-bye to Marcelle nor does she know what the parting words were. She believes her father offered to take Marcelle because of the distance to the school and because of the heavy suitcase she was carrying. She does not believe Marcelle or Mr. Devries initiated the requested.

According to ME, her father spoke with Mr. Devries prior to the August 24th issuance of the summons and offered to hide Mr. Devries, Mrs. Devries, and Marcelle. However, according to ME, Mr. Devries rejected the offer; the stated reason was his concern the family home would be lost were the family to leave Maastricht.

ME used the word *sacrifice* to describe the decision; when clarification was requested, she was very clear that Mr. Devries sacrificed Marcelle in the hope this would ensure the family maintain the home.

One week after Marcelle's deportation, Mr. and Mrs. Devries were forced to leave the home and move to the factory where they lived in difficult conditions until they went into hiding. When Mr. Devries requested her father's assistance in facilitating his and Mrs. Devries' escape, Mr. Eurling refused. His refusal was based on his anger at their previous rejection of his offer to help all three family members escape together.

When Mr. Devries returned to Maastricht after the war, he was not popular with the Eurlings, because it was believed he placed greater priority on preserving ownership of the family home than on ensuring the safety of his daughter.

On June 2, 2016, Professor Grunfeld and I retraced Marcelle's journey. Although there have been some changes in Maastricht's roads over the past decades and some uncertainty exists regarding specific turns Mr. Eurling made, our retracing, according to Professor Grunfeld, accurately depicts their route.

The retracing sheds light on what townspeople would have seen when Marcelle was taken to the school and, later that evening, when she walked to the train station. The issue is relevant to the bystander question.

The mid-day journey—we do not know exactly what time—from Marcelle's house to the school was through residential and business areas alike. It is assumed there was nothing unusual about a man and woman on a horse-carriage; there was no reason Mr. Eurling and Marcelle would have drawn attention to themselves. That is distinct from L's observation of many Jews walking, carrying their luggage, toward the school.[10]

However, the Devries' neighbors could have observed Mr. Eurling and Marcelle as they set off on the trip from the Devries' home. There is no indication Mr. and Mrs. Devries accompanied Marcelle to the horse-carriage. We do not know if there was any interaction with the neighbors or any last-minute efforts to facilitate Marcelle's going into hiding.

If there were such attempts, they tragically went unheeded. We do know that some people, including Mr. Eurling, Mr. Salamon,[11] and others,[12] had knowledge of the summons prior to its delivery on August 24.

It is assumed there was nothing remarkable about the journey to the school; we do not know what, if anything, Mr. Eurling and Marcelle discussed. Our conversation with ME did not shed light on this matter. What we do know is that Mr. Eurling brought Marcelle and returned thereafter. His anger with Mr. Devries is referenced above.

---

10. See p. 146.
11. See p. 144–145.
12. See L.S., p. 146.

The short walk from the school to the train station occurred around 10 p.m. Because of existing regulations, house lights were dimmed (turned off) in order to hamper Allied forces' aerial bombing on occupied Germany. Furthermore, Maastricht residents were not allowed to be in the city streets after 8 p.m. and were ordered to blacken their windows.

As a result, the short walk to the train station was conducted, literally, under the stealth of darkness. This is relevant as it strongly suggests the final walk went unobserved; this was reinforced in a conversation with B whose childhood home was across the street from the school.

We do not know how many soldiers were present and if there was any resistance. However, based on extensive interviews, it is assumed the 250 Jews carrying their luggage walked quietly and peacefully to the train station, not imposing a burden on the German soldiers.

Deportation, the Bystander, and City Residents

The deportation of Maastricht's Jews can be viewed from four distinct perspectives—before the sending of the summons, the decision upon receiving the summons on August 24 whether to report to the school or go into hiding, the daytime walk to the school, and the nighttime walk to the train station.

Regarding the nighttime walk, it is a certainty that Maastricht residents were not present. At this very late stage, the fate of the 290 Jews walking from the school to the train station was sealed.

That is distinct from the first three stages. That conclusion is based both on the number of Jews who went into hiding prior to the issuance of the summons and the number who chose to ignore it. Separating the four stages into two distinct elements facilitates the bystander discussion: In stage four, there was no opportunity to intervene-interfere in the deportation process—the opportunity existed in stages 1 through 3.

The daytime walk was observed; the question is whether efforts were made to encourage Jews to go into hiding at this stage and what the response was to the offer. I have found no evidence regarding offers made during the walk nor reactions. That is, however, not to say offers were not made.

What of offers to provide safety before the summons was issued or on the day it was issued?

We know approximately 150 Jews decided to ignore the summons and go into hiding; we do not know how many such offers were actually made. However, by analyzing the action of one family, we have insight regarding the decision-making process upon receipt of the summons.

From Dr. Herman van Rees I learned the following:[13]

The Silber family had six members: Mr. Silber, Mrs. Silber and four sons, Salamon (a student, 19 years old), Max (who fixed cars, 18 years old), Chanine (a student, 16 years old) and Aaron (a student, 12 years old). Mr. Silber was over 60 years old, Mrs. Silber was infirm and Aaron was under 15 years of age and they received an exemption from the August 24th Summons.

Upon receipt of the Summons, a Calvinist Priest offered the family to "dive." That evening, the family discussed how to respond regarding Salamon, Chanine and Aaron; the question was whether to dive or report. The assumption was that reporting was dangerous given the belief that many people will do in Labor camps[14] where hard physical work is demanded.

Of the three brothers, Max both was the strongest and had a skill— car repair—that was relevant to the Germans. Therefore, the family decided Salamon and Chanine would go into hiding and Max would report for transport on August 25th.

On August 25th Max took leave of his family; according to Salamon's diary, as Max began the 15 minute walk to the School carrying his luggage, the family emotionally parted from him while standing in the street.

In contrast to the 24 hour period between Summons and the requirement to report, the second deportation in Maastricht, November 1942, reflected "lessons learned" as Jews were not given time to

---

13. Dr. van Rees' discussion was, in large part, based on Salamon Silber's diary.
14. The reader will recall my father was in a labor (mining) camp for just short of six months (June to November 1944).

report. Rather, policemen knocked on their doors ordering them to quickly gather their belongings and report immediately for deportation. In April 1943, upon reading in a newspaper of the impending third deportation,[15] Mr. and Mrs. Silber went into hiding. Akin to the family discussion on August 24th, the Silbers had time to consider their decision and options.

Max who was sent to a concentration camp, survived the Holocaust as did his siblings and parents.

The three deportations in Maastricht—August 1942, November 1942, and April 1943—were carried out in different manners. That is important for our purposes. In August 1942 and April 1943 Jews were given time to decide whether to report as ordered or go into hiding. If they chose the former, there was time to pack their belongings in accordance with the summons.

As we have learned, different families made different decisions—some resulting in tragedy, others in survival. Those who survived were clearly helped by others; the decision to "dive" required active assistance whether from the resistance, friends, or family.

However, these three categories are not akin to the bystander—quite the opposite. That is, the act of hiding was not the result of random acts of assistance or kindness offered by a stranger at the moment the victim was confronted with impending deportation.

What is of interest to us is whether Maastricht residents—when watching the town's Jews, accompanied by Dutch policemen, carrying their luggage—offered to provide a hiding place at the "last moment." The image of a group of Jews, wearing Yellow Stars, carrying luggage, and walking in the direction of the Central Train Station must have left no doubt in people's minds that danger loomed. That is true whether they knew of the summons or not.

Although there was concern regarding the risk attendant to being a "hider," statistics indicate that fear was significantly overestimated. However, that was not known at the time. In addition, as was repeatedly noted, the Dutch ethos is predicated on a combination of accommodation,

---

15. See the conversation with L.S. regarding her father, pp. 146–147.

obedience, and respect for authority. That ethos, undoubtedly, was reinforced by the knowledge of the brutal punishment meted out to those participating in the 1941 strike.[16]

The near-certain cruel death that awaited those sent to Mauthausen was a powerful deterrent. However, 25,000 Jews did go into hiding of which 15,000 survived; while the exact number of hiders is unknown, one scholar suggested that number required approximately 50,000 Dutch citizens to be involved in the effort to assist their fellow citizens.

Nevertheless, and the "but" is the essence of the bystander discussion, these individuals were *not* bystanders. They were, in large part, members of an organized resistance, largely, but not exclusively, non-Jewish. The bystander watching the procession in the overwhelming majority of cases did not offer assistance; as we have come to learn, offers to go into hiding in Maastricht were made by neighbors and members of the resistance.

These were not random offers but rather in response to a summons to report. There is a sharp distinction between the two; the bystander did not come to the assistance of Maastricht's Jews.

Saving Yourself: Explaining Bystander Action or Inaction

Measures, otherwise unacceptable, perhaps unfathomable in normal circumstances, are legitimate in an effort to save yourself. That is, when confronting the unimaginable, a significant broadening of tolerable behavior is perceived as acceptable. That is not to imply illegal behavior is to be encouraged but does suggest conduct otherwise morally on or, perhaps, over the edge, is recognized as situationally legitimate.

There is, of course, risk in this perspective for it suggests tolerating what would be, otherwise, intolerable. The risk is such an approach that it potentially enables criminal conduct in the face of life-threatening circumstances.

By way of analogy, if the law this book proposes were in effect, would an exception be made for L.S.' father? After all, when the neighbors were

---

16. https://www.popularresistance.org/on-this-day-in-1941-anti-nazi-february-strike-in-holland/.

deported he was a single parent, raising seven children. Would those circumstances absolve him of criminal, not moral, responsibility and accountability? Are there particular circumstances that justify acting in contravention to a law?

The question is one of exceptions and the extent of tolerable "wiggle room." There are three distinct ways to approach this question—draft legislation that does not tolerate exceptions, draft legislation with clearly defined circumstances that tolerate exceptions, and draft legislation that tolerates exceptions without precise definition of circumstances that tolerate exceptions.

Posing this question raises the question of implementability of the particular legislation. This, obviously, requires the cooperation of law enforcement, prosecutors, and the judiciary. However, it is the legislature that must draft laws in a manner that enables reasonable application. The exceptions discussion is of great importance for it forces us to confront, and resolve, the extent to which legislation will be, in actuality, applied.

The conversations in Maastricht brought this issue to the fore.

I was humbled people were willing to share their stories and experiences; this is, as a friend insightfully noted, both a privilege and a burden. The privilege is the willingness to share with me; the burden is to honestly capture the essence of the story.

The stories were powerful and compelling. All reflected complexity, pain, and human suffering raising endless questions. The conversations, individually and collectively, powerfully reinforced the inherent risk in relying on people doing the "right thing."

Although approximately 11 percent[17] of Limburg's Jews went into hiding of which 90 percent survived, bystanders were not involved in the hiding process.[18] Rather, it was family, friends, and the organized resistance responsible for providing Jews haven. That, for me, puts the lie to

---

17. 170 out of 1,500.

18. Although the overwhelming majority of those involved in hiding Jews were brave and well intentioned, I also learned of painful stories of abuse and harm caused to children in hiding. A sobering and moving conversation with G highlighted the risk of separating children from parents and siblings from siblings.

While the rationale for doing so is understandable, the consequences could be significant. A child in hiding is vulnerable and dependent; in those instances, there were—given the circumstances—evidentially no bystanders who could provide assistance.

the argument that people will do the right thing; those who participated in efforts to hide Jews were not bystanders.

The intersection between victim and bystander—merely watching than actually helpful—has been captured in many photographs. Actually, intersection suggests a meeting; in reality, the more correct metaphor is a parallel universe of two individuals in profoundly different circumstances. The decision not to meet at the intersection is that of the bystanders; the victim cannot bring the bystander to the intersection, whereas the bystander can bring the victim there.

When looking at pictures from the Holocaust my focus is neither the perpetrator nor victim.[19] Rather, I try to visualize what the bystander saw and understood. Looking at the pictures in this manner raises the following questions:

1. Where does the bystander think the Jews are going?
2. What does the bystander see when looking at Jews boarding buses and trucks?
3. If standing or sitting on a balcony and observing Jews carrying luggage walking toward a train station, what is the reasonable assumption regarding their destination?
4. Is the person the bystander is observing a "Jew" or "Dutch" or a "Dutch Jew"?
5. How does the presence of authority—soldier or police officer—impact the bystander's perception?
6. What does the bystander know?
7. How is time to act-respond relevant?
8. What are the bystander's capabilities?
9. Who else is in a position to assist?

We, of course, do not have answers to these questions. After all, bystanders do not volunteer that they were present and chose not to act. Rather, and perhaps understandably, they do not see themselves as

---

19. In June 2016 I reviewed a significant number of Holocaust pictures when visiting the Wannsee Conference Center; the staff—under the leadership of Dr. Hans-Christian Bosch—were extraordinarily helpful and unfailingly gracious in facilitating my research. The visit was follow-up to a previous visit, July 2015; see p. 21.

positioned to have acted. From their perspective they were, at best, present when something happened. Perhaps they were present but somehow did not see even though they were there.

Bystanders can hide behind the uncertainty of a particular situation; in addition, trying to understand a particular situation may result in unintended involvement. That is, the bystander may be dragged into an event-incident-situation.

Therefore, for the overwhelming majority of bystanders, nonintervention is the safe course of action. From the victim's perspective, that passivity, whether as observer or spectator, facilitates the perpetrator's capability to cause harm.

The concept of being present but refraining from involvement on behalf of the victim suggests Maastricht's Gentiles' perception of Jews walking to the school. The three-part notion of uniformity, naturalized customs of everyday life, and a desire to fit into mainstream society are essential to understanding bystander conduct.[20]

The notion of mainstream society is particularly important; by analogy, the following is particularly insightful in helping us understand Maastricht's Gentiles:

The year 1938—with the annexation of Austria and the Reich-wide anti-Jewish November pogroms (Kristalnacht, ANG)—definitively ended all illusions Jews may have had for a future in Germany.[21]

The poet Edward Yashinsky movingly wrote: "Fear only the indifferent who permit the killers and betrayers to walk safely on the earth."[22]

Fearing the "indifferent" is a powerful articulation of the bystander; it captures the act of ignoring the victim's peril. It powerfully presents the reality that the bystander is aware of the danger, yet decides to ignore it.

---

20. I draw on Professor Baum's work; Steven K. Baum, *The Psychology of Genocide, Perpetrators, Bystanders and Rescuers*, Cambridge University Press, Cambridge, 2008.
21. *Bystanders, Rescuers or Perpetrators: The Neutral Countries and the South*, p. 26, http://www.hsozkult.de/conferencereport/id/tagungsberichte-5829.
22. Steven K. Baum, *The Psychology of Genocide, Perpetrators, Bystanders and Rescuers*, p. 154, http://www.quotehd.com/quotes/author/edward-yashinsky-poet-quotes.

The reason or reasons for doing so are varied—the notion of outside "mainstream" society is particularly illuminating in understanding the bystander's motivation. However, from the victim's perspective, regardless of the motivation(s) for nonintervention, the consequence is the same—harm to the victim the bystander could have minimized. That is how I understand Yashinsky's warning.

A straight line can be drawn between bystander indifference and victim harm. That is not to diminish the primary role of the perpetrator; after all, the basis—the underpinning for the victim's precariousness—is the perpetrator, not the bystander. However, the bystander's complicity—what Yashinsky termed "indifferent"—facilitates the perpetrator's action and enables impending harm to the victim.

We momentarily digress; according to Professor David Bankier:

> [T]he vast number of testimonies given during and after the war by both Germans and Jews, as well as contemporaries' diaries, lead to the conclusion that large sections of the German population, both Jews and non-Jews either knew or suspected what was happening in Poland and Russia. A few testimonies illustrate this contention. One survivor commented that in December 1942 he did not know about gassing but suspected that death was awaiting the Jewish deportees . . . Viennese Jews were openly mentioning that deportation meant starvation or being shot in a grave they would dig themselves.[23]

Regarding deportations in Vienna we learn from the diary of Ludwig Haydn:

> The aged who could not walk were put on trucks while seated on their chairs. As to the reactions to the expulsion, most people looked away, ashamed; others laughed and enjoyed the view.[24]
> The round-up (of Jews to Auschwitz on February 27, 1943, from Berlin) was accompanied by strife and beatings, but apart from those

---

23. David Bankier, *The Germans and the Final Solution: Public Opinion Under Nazism*, Blackwell, Oxford, 1992, p. 103.
24. Ibid., p. 132.

directly concerned and the few who dared to tell the Gestapo men to go fight on the front and leave old Jews alone, most observers . . . were completely indifferent.[25]

According to Bankier, Professor Martin Broszat, an expert on Nazi Germany, wrote:

"The passive and apathetic responses of the German public were not merely incidental, but were motivated by people's awareness of being accomplices who shared responsibility for crimes."[26]

The above quotes address the "knowledge" question: When did people know the fate that awaited European Jewry? That question has been the subject of intensive academic inquiry over the past decades. It is not my intention to address the broader historical debate; what is relevant to the bystander question is what did the individual know and more importantly, or at least of equal relevance, what did the bystander see.

More narrowly, what did the bystander choose to see? The relevant follow-up question is whether choosing not to see frees the bystander from complicity; that is, does deliberate ignorance acquit you of criminal liability?

This takes us back to the pictures: I refer back to them because they are so integral to understanding the physicality of the bystander-victim relationship and the resulting legal complicity arising from that "interaction." The use of the quotes is deliberate because, in the overwhelming majority of time, there was no interaction.

Perhaps there was a glance; perhaps there was an avoidance of glancing. Whichever it was, the victim remained vulnerable to the intentions of the perpetrator. Simply put, the bystander was complicit in that harm. In examining thousands of Holocaust pictures I am struck that oftentimes the victim did not look at the bystander.

I found this particularly to be the case regarding pictures of Jews being marched to the train station. In the main, they were looking straight ahead, carrying their luggage, glancing neither left nor right. It is also

---

25. Ibid., p. 136.
26. Ibid., p. 145.

striking how few persons of authority can be seen accompanying them. This is different from pictures at train platforms which appear very crowded with policeman and victims.

The pictures I have examined reflect very few bystanders at the train station; this suggests the last opportunity for bystander intervention is when Jews arrived at the train station. The pictures depict a significant range in number of bystanders; in some marches there were few bystanders, in others there many bystanders standing on sidewalks or sitting on balconies.

Were they indifferent? Were they criminals? Did they fail morally? This leaves us with the proposal to criminalize complicity.

The Holocaust pictures are a most compelling argument supporting the recommendation; conversations in Maastricht reinforced what pictures convey. The combination of the two—eyewitnesses and pictures—is powerful support for the recommendation.

However, caution and care are important. Criminalizing complicity rightfully raises concern. Is this an exception-free proposal? The question is not posed abstractly but rather concretely: Can a counterargument not be made that individual circumstances and general conditions alike must give pause before prosecuting the bystander?

I refer back to L.S.' painfully candid recounting of her father's inaction.[27] Even if one accepts her term "coward," do his difficult personal circumstances not justify an exception to defining him a criminal? The term *coward* does not suggest guilt but does reflect the father could have done more. It is assumed the father's decision making was significantly influenced by his own circumstances: a single parent raising seven children.

L.S.' comment regarding her father led to a vigorous exchange with friends and colleagues. All were moved by her candor; most were uncomfortable with possible prosecution of her father given the family's extenuating circumstances. That is, the seven children under his care were suggested as an exception to the proposed rule. The underpinning for the recommendation regarding an exception was the argument that

---

27. See pp. 146–147.

in certain situations it is legitimate to act counter to what is otherwise expected or demanded.

The argument is understandable and reasonable; however, it must be balanced against legislative intent and social policy. We must weigh the question based on what the father knew, rather than what we know today. As previously discussed, those who provided assistance to Jews in Maastricht were, overwhelmingly, not harmed by the authorities. It is safe to assume that the father did not know this on April 9, 1943.

How much time did he have to make his decision? From what L.S. conveyed, the "act-don't act" window was very brief; probably a couple of minutes. However, that is longer than an instinctual decision to dive into a swimming pool to save a drowning child. The question of acting in contravention to accepted norms in extreme circumstances was an issue I discussed with MP.

MP's grandmother was a prisoner in Auschwitz; in January 1945 she participated in one of the most famous Death Marches when the Nazis decided to close the camp in the face of the rapidly approaching Russian Army. When the Death March began there was no known or articulated destination; the marchers walked through the same town a number of times.

The march was led by soldiers as many of the camp commanders had escaped, hoping to avoid the wrath of the Russians. On May 8, 1945, MP's grandmother wrote an extraordinary letter to her family from Sweden. When she wrote the letter she did not know if her two children (MP's mother and uncle) were alive or not.

MP graciously allowed me to include portions of the letter below. Although the letter references her grandmother's experience on the Death March, I suggest it is relevant to the bystander discussion.

> *I start (this part of my letter) at the evacuation. I was selected by the Gestapo commander and the Standortartz to take care of a special Häftling. During the time I was waiting for this patient (f) I slept for one month all alone in a room that was warmed day and night. The 18th of January at 5 a.m. I was quietly cleaning my room, as a friend came asking me if I was going to be crazy. We should evacuated. Ima, a 24 years old sweet girl, and I stayed in the Lager until 9 p.m. The*

Germans burned all the paper and gave us some food. Of course—as always—the Polish and Russian women got most of the food, so many of our women had to leave with nothing. Ima and I had each if us two loaves of bread, a tin of meat, a tin of margarine and some sugar. In this way we went on through the snow. Two hours later the Russians arrived. We were walking during one night and three days in the snow. Along the road a lot of men and women lay exhausted and with bashed heads. The worst thing is that all of us have changed so heavily, that we abandoned our values to examine whether the dead bodies had something useful to ourselves.

In the first half of an hour I already had throwed away my blanket. This all was too heavy for me, and I only wanted to live and to see again my children, if God at least had saved them. Every day we ate 3 slices of bread. After that we were transported 3 days and 3 nights in open cattle trucks and had only some snow for drinking. Every night many people died in the train. The fourth day we arrived in Ravensbrück.[28]

---

28. The complete letter is published (in Dutch) in Marja Pinckaers, *De cirkel; hommage aan Marie Hertzdahl-Bloemgarten*. Valkenburg, the Netherlands, 2011, pp. 56–57.

— 9 —

Hungary: The Ultimate Bystander?

Introduction

I came to Hungary in June 2016 with mixed feelings. For me, it was looking at the Holocaust directly, eyeball to eyeball. I cannot examine Hungary objectively or abstractly. That would be an unreasonable expectation by reader and writer alike. It is, in many ways, my Heart of Darkness.

The Hungary of today does not interest me; I have no skin in the game. Friends who have been here repeatedly comment on Budapest's charm and beauty, noting how much they enjoyed themselves. I have no doubt that is the case. However, I did not come to Budapest interested in today's Hungary. Walking the streets of Budapest has no significance for me. My sole focus is the Hungary that murdered my grandparents, sent my father to Bor, and sought to murder my mother.

Not only did my parents never discuss the Holocaust, Hungary was a nontopic in my childhood. My knowledge of Hungarian culture, literature, history, politics, and society is extremely limited, focused on a very specific time period.

Frankly, I have no interest in knowing anything about contemporary Hungary and Hungarians. Whether to my credit or not is beside the point; it is the reality. My week-long visit was functional and utilitarian, focused on one issue.

My sole intent was to better understand specific events relevant to my family—meetings conducted, places visited, and material research centered on issues this book addresses. Friends and colleagues suggested I was, metaphorically, witness to events of over seventy years ago. For me, honoring the memory of my grandparents and better understanding the world of my parents was all that mattered to me.

To achieve this required going back in time.

A Holocaust survivor with whom I met described the ten-month period—March 19, 1944,[1] to January 18, 1945[2]—as madness and cruelty, compounded by deep anti-Semitism.

That ten-month period is the only reason I visit Hungary.

These events occurred while Hungary was under German occupation; nevertheless, the breadth and depth of Hungarian cooperation was extraordinary. Scholars have suggested the Holocaust in Hungary be divided into three periods:

1. March 19, 1944–July 9, 1944: The period of deportations under German control with Hungarian collaboration and complicity
2. July 1944–October 15, 1944: The period of no deportations
3. October 15, 1944–March 28, 1945: The period after the Arrow Cross overthrows the Horthy government in a coup d'état and undertakes the destruction of Budapest Jewry

The Arrow Cross was the Hungarian Fascist Party, faithfully pro-Nazi, responsible for the deportation and murder of Budapest Jews.[3]

The Russian occupation of Budapest saved Budapest's Jews from the fate of those living outside Hungary's capital. That is not to diminish or minimize the suffering of Budapest's Jews in that three-month period.

---

1. German occupation of Hungary.
2. Russian liberation of Budapest.
3. http://www.yadvashem.org/odot_pdf/Microsoft%20Word%20-%205756.pdf.

The Courtyard

I went to the wall where my mother was lined up to be shot with her mother. The wall is in a courtyard; standing there was both overwhelming and sobering. I assumed seeing the place would be difficult; I had prepared myself, as much as one can, for such a place. However, there is a difference between the preparation and the actual. On my previous trip to Budapest, with my father, we had gone to the building's entrance but not inside to the courtyard.

Entrance to the courtyard.

The courtyard is crucial on two different levels—physical and existential.[4] The former because this is, after all, where the forces of evil fully intended to kill my mother; the latter because of the confluence it represents between evil and survival.[5] While she, thankfully, survived, there is nothing good about the building: It manifests the Holocaust's sheer madness in general, Hungary in particular.

The Hungarian Arrow Cross's—not German soldiers'—determined effort to destroy Budapest Jewry is the essence of what was about to unfold in the courtyard:

> *More sinister activity, however, was taking place throughout the city. In early December, about seventy thousand of Budapest's approximately 140,000 Jews were rounded up by Hungarian gendarmes and Arrow Cross fascists under Gestapo supervision and herded into a large ghetto in central Pest. Those left behind stayed in hiding or lived precariously in a smaller "international ghetto," which was in reality less protected than the enclosed central ghetto. It was during this time that the heroic Swedish emissary Raoul Wallenberg made his name by resorting to every means possible—Red Cross and Swedish government passes, real and forged, cajolery, bribery, and reckless courage—to save as many of Budapest's Jews as possible. What made Budapest unusual was that due to relatively benign Hungarian policies against the Jews preceding the German occupation in March 1944, the city was the only remaining urban area anywhere within Nazi-occupied Europe that had a substantial surviving Jewish population by December 1944.[6]*

Those Arrow Cross members seconds away from pulling the trigger were perpetrators; they had my mother and grandmother fully in their sight lines, standing but yards away. The intention was to kill them. The Arrow Cross was conducting similar attacks on a nightly basis in Budapest, whether in courtyards, in the streets, or on the banks of the

---

4. A friend suggested the word; upon reflection it accurately captures and reflects much of the emotion.
5. Primo Levi's writings are particularly relevant on this issue.
6. http://www.historynet.com/world-war-ii-siege-of-budapest.htm.

Danube. Jewish blood flowed through the Danube; the extraordinary shoe memorial is testimony to this.[7]

There is no doubt who were the perpetrators and who were victims. Similarly, it is clear who were the rescuers—young Jews[8] roaming the streets of Budapest at night in stolen Arrow Cross uniforms trying to save Jews seconds away from their deaths at the hands of the Arrow Cross. It was a ruse; sometimes it worked, sometimes not. In my mother's case, it did.

The building is comprised of three floors surrounding the courtyard. I do not know what the building's physical condition was seventy years ago; similarly, I do not know what the relationship was between Jewish and Gentile neighbors. What I do know is that a Gentile woman brought my mother and grandmother food and Gentile neighbors ratted them out.

The former is a Righteous Gentile; the latter perpetrators, not bystanders; they are the essence of collaborators. Their complicity goes well beyond bystander complicity. In the madness of the ten-month period—at the very moment the Arrow Cross intended to kill my mother—her life hung in tenuous balance. The "live-die" question could only be resolved by the active intervention of someone—of anyone.

There was no one to call; the forces of evil were the authorities. In the courtyard with armed Arrow Cross members aiming their guns, seconds away from opening fire, there was need for immediate intervention. This was, literally, a life-death scenario with no time to spare. Intervention had to be immediate.

Standing inside the courtyard on a Saturday afternoon seventy-two years after the fact illuminated this reality. There is, literally, no place to hide. There are no nooks, no crannies, no hidden corners. The physicality is stark: It is an enclosed space, the distance from one end to the other is not far.

I do not know against which wall my mother and grandmother were lined up. I can but try to imagine the overwhelming fear and sense of

---

7. http://visitbudapest.travel/articles/one-of-budapests-most-moving-memorials-shoes-on-the-danube/.

8. https://www.amazon.com/Brothers-Resistance-Rescue-Underground-Movement/dp/9652293865/ref=sr_1_fkmr1_1?ie=UTF8&qid=1465794122&sr=8-1-fkmr1&keywords=PROFESSOR+DAVID+GUR.

utter helplessness and hopelessness. Four walls, a courtyard, and madness and evil manifested by your fellow countrymen.

My mother and grandmother were no less Hungarian than those about to shoot them. They were not interlopers from another country. My mother's family were Hungarian citizens, no different than Arrow Cross followers intent on destroying Budapest Jewry. The destruction of Budapest Jewry was a mission the Arrow Cross took upon itself; this was not an "order" from the Germans to be implemented by Hungarians.[9]

Once outed by a neighbor, once ordered to the courtyard, once standing in the courtyard facing immediate death, a 12-year-old child's life is in the hands of others. There are three options:[10]

1. The perpetrator will decide not to act.
2. A bystander will intervene.
3. Rescuers (distinct from bystanders) will appear.

Who were the bystanders? According to my mother:

[A]t about five o'clock in the afternoon, (on October 19, 1944) it was getting dark, we heard shouting below, calling us down to the courtyard. . . . Mother and I went down the steps, she holding a small bag in one hand and my hand in the other. As we reached the courtyard where all the others were gathered, we were pushed against a wall and told to be quiet. I was terrified, not knowing what to expect but somehow aware that something terrible was going to happen.[11]

My hotel in Budapest is located a short walk from the building where my mother lived. While unintended, the juxtaposition has significance for me. It accentuates the reality—retroactively, of course—of the events described in her essay.

There is a power to be so close to the physical location, albeit separated by decades and worlds. However, that does not minimize the power of

---

9. Distinct from deportation of Hungarian Jewry, March 1944–June 1944.
10. I do not believe in "divine intervention."
11. http://www.bjpa.org/Publications/downloadFile.cfm?FileID=17080.

the question at hand: What could we reasonably have expected of the neighbors looking out the window and seeing fellow neighbors about to be shot?

The question is could the neighbors have acted? Did they have an interest in acting? With whom were their sympathies aligned? What was the risk in providing assistance to my mother and grandmother?

Hungarian scholars with whom I met emphasized that most civilians in Budapest in the fall of 1944 were women, children, the elderly, and the infirm; able-bodied men were fully engaged in the war effort. To confront the Arrow Cross—well armed, extremely violent, virulently anti-Semitic, and not fully subject to a traditional chain of command—was extremely risky under such circumstances. That is important to consider when weighing the actions-inactions of the neighbors.

What is clear is that the neighbors were a mixed bag: On the one hand, there was at least one neighbor who brought them food; on the other hand, there was at least one neighbor who turned on them. The motivations of each are unknown to me; ramifications and consequences could not have been more disparate. One sustains life; the other directly contributes to its brutal end. The former is a rescuer; the latter a perpetrator.

Neither are passive and disengaged. Quite the opposite: Both take concrete measures that directly impact the lives of two individuals. I assume the elderly woman saw my mother and grandmother as victims; the informing neighbor, it is to be presumed, understood them to be the enemy.

According to my mother "it was getting dark." I take that to mean a curious neighbor could see outside. It was not dark. This is different from Marcelle Devries' walk at night, along with 250 other Jews, from the school to Maastricht's train station. Whether neighbors heard the commotion is difficult to assess; history is replete with examples of people choosing neither to see nor hear.

Some have been discussed in this book. What could the neighbors have done? Rearticulated, is it possible that the dire circumstances my mother and grandmother faced presented no viable option for bystanders to intervene?

The answer to that depends on how we define the bystander.

June 14, 2016

I had planned to visit my father's hometown on his birthday (June 13) but because of the Jewish holiday of Shavuot there was a need to postpone by one day. I intended to visit the Jewish cemetery where there is a memorial to the town's Holocaust victims, to go to the Ministry of Interior to verify my father's childhood address, to go to the town archivist to research Holocaust material, to go to the family home and then to retrace my grandparents' walk from home to train station.

The above were accomplished.[12] The day was difficult, occasionally brutal. The Holocaust and the price paid by my family hit me full force in the stomach. Standing in front of the memorial, with my grandparents' names, was deeply moving. When I said the Kaddish[13] there was a sense of deep connection to two people I never met.

My father's home (renovated over the years).

---

12. With many thanks to Karesz Vandor, Hungarian Jewish genealogist, Hungarian Roots.
13. http://www.jewishvirtuallibrary.org/jsource/Judaism/kaddish.html.

A UEI UNIALAS UIUDIN EVFORDULOJAN

BUCHSBAUM SAMU NYÍRGELSE
BUCHSBAUM SAMUNÉ
BUCHSBAUM MIKLÓS
BECK HENRIK DEMECSER
BECK HENRIKNÉ
BECK KATALIN
GOLDBERG S. ÉS
GOLDBERG TERÉZ
FARKAS MÁRTON
FARKAS KATALIN
WEISZ JENÖ
WEISZ BERTA
WEISZ ERNÖ
ÖZV. KLEIN MÁRKUSNÉ
ÖZV. FRIEDMAN GYULÁNÉ
SCHWARTZ ADOLF
SCHWARTZ ADOLFNÉ
GOTTESMAN HERMAN
GOTTESMAN RÓZSI

The memorial.

The memorial is stark and graceful; the list of names is endless. I stood there for a long time, staring at my grandparents' names. I am pained that we have no picture of my grandfather who dared to defy his father-in-law and sent my father and uncle to Budapest. I owe him my life.

Although there is no grave to visit, the memorial is sufficiently powerful. The cemetery is well maintained; it is simple and stark. The quiet is overwhelming; the sense of loss beyond words.

Looking for a very long time, staring at their names, I had many thoughts running through my mind. I thought of the remarkable life my father created in the aftermath of the Holocaust, I thought of my grandparents' last moments on earth as they stood in the selection line in Auschwitz, I thought of my three children in Israel, and I realized how important it is for me to directly confront evil.

I asked myself what is the connection between the memorial and this book. The answer was very clear: There is no room for inaction. The price is simply too high. The memorial conveys that, at least for me.

At the cemetery, by prior arrangement, I met with a woman whose mother was deported with my grandparents. My grandparents and this woman's parents lived on the same street, separated by a couple of blocks. The woman shared with me what her mother told her regarding the neighbors' conduct when the families walked to the train station.

Because my grandparents' house was inside the Jewish ghetto—it was at its outer wall—they did not need to leave their house when the ghetto was established in the aftermath of the German occupation of Hungary. Due to its location, it is safe to assume some Jews who moved into the ghetto lived with my grandparents until their deportation.

As to the neighbors, as my grandparents, and others, walked to the train station they were spat on, swore at, and hit. I was, frankly, not surprised to learn this. I did not have any expectation to learn something different. It fits accounts I have read elsewhere; I do not think my father would be surprised to learn this were he alive. It largely fits the motif he shared with me.

The recounting filled me with sadness more than anger. I wondered why not offer neighbors carrying their meager belongings dignified words of parting, if not actual assistance.

Was this nothing more than mean-spirited anti-Semitism? Were the neighbors happy the town Jews were leaving? Was there a sense of an opportunity to benefit from their departure? After all, houses, property, furniture, clothing, and other belongings would soon be available. Were there decades-long grudges and resentments?

We do not know the answers to these questions.

However, we can presume with a reasonable degree of certainty the behavior reflects a combination of motivations. The bottom line is that offers of assistance were not made as the Jews walked to the train station. Help was not forthcoming. The memorial at the cemetery makes that abundantly clear.

In May 1944 there was little doubt what fate awaited those walking to the train station. The neighbor is the classic bystander facing three options:

1. Offer assistance.
2. Do nothing.
3. Contribute to victim travail.

My grandparents' neighbors chose the third option. That is obvious.

Is that a crime as articulated in this book? The neighbors did not make the situation worse; humiliation and taunting, while morally disgraceful, are not crimes. Were the neighbors complicit? In the broad, collective sense of the word, the answer is yes. In the individual—legally accountable and liable—application of the phrase, maybe?

Unlike other bystanders examined in this book who claimed "did not see-did not hear," these neighbors chose to actively engage. Unfortunately, that engagement was, from the victim's perspective, most unhelpful. Although taunting is not a crime, hitting another individual is clearly an assault. That is a crime. Of that, there should be no doubt. In essence, my grandparents' neighbors transitioned from bystander to perpetrator. That is a punishable offense in any legal system.

I ended my day painfully.

The walk from their house concluded at the train station. I stood outside trying to imagine what their thoughts were. I looked around before entering the station. I quickly walked through the station. It had no special importance for me. That is very distinct from the train platform.

The platform.

I stood on the platform fully cognizant this is where my grandparents stood before boarding the train to Auschwitz. Although the station has been renovated over the years, the platform has not. This was the platform.

The tracks seemed endless. The trains at the station were not the modern trains of modern-day Germany and the Netherlands—quite the opposite. There was a sense these trains were from another age. The tracks, the platform, and the trains were an overwhelmingly powerful reminder of why I have undertaken this project.

I have looked at an endless number of train platform pictures over the past four years. Standing on the same platform my grandparents stood minutes before deportation to Auschwitz, the sense of loss for people I never met was overwhelming.

My day began where it ended—with the murder of my grandparents.

In the morning a somber and sobering visit to the memorial with their names inscribed; in the afternoon standing on *the* platform. This would not have happened without the bystander; when retracking their journey from house to train station I was very cognizant of the endless opportunities for assistance, respite, and a kind word. Those were not forthcoming. Their fate was doomed.

June 15, 2016

On June 15, 2016, I visited my father's school.

It was the most appropriate way to finish my three-week, three-country intensive study of the bystander. The school, much like the courtyard, is directly related both to my parents' Holocaust experiences and to the bystander.

My father's school.

Prior to the trip I took to Hungary in March 2000 with my father, he wrote me the following regarding the school:

A different universe altogether (compared to school in his hometown, ANG). Ten bright kids in a class, taught by highly qualified, sometimes brilliant, teachers lay and clerical . . . the seminary (School, ANG) was an intellectually stimulating and, in an increasingly hostile outside world, sheltered environment. It was also a source of pride, like esprit de corps . . .

It all came crashing down on Sunday, March 19, 1944 when SS. Obersturmbahnfuhrer Eichmann's people entered the building (in fact surprising us in our classroom) and turned our school into a concentration camp for the "prominente."[14]

As I have come to learn in interactions with Hungarian scholars, there are many reasons—quoting my father—that it came "crashing down." Many actors—German and Hungarian alike—bear responsibility for the events of March 1944–March 1945. What stands out is the remarkable dedication to destroying Hungarian Jewry while conducting military battles unrelated to Final Solution implementation.

The decision to initially deport Jews living in northeast Hungary reflected military realities: The expectation was that major battles would take place against Russian forces coming from the east. This was a clear race against time. To deport 450,000 Jews in less than sixty days required significant cooperation and collaboration.

The Germans received that cooperation and collaboration: 52,000 Hungarian civil servants and 200,000 Hungarians participated in this effort. The number of "Jewish experts" Eichmann brought with him, between 60 and 200, was numerically insignificant in comparison. Not by chance was it suggested to me that the Hungarians did not need Eichmann to deport their fellow countrymen.

They were fully capable, according to some, of undertaking this effort without external assistance. The 50,000 German soldiers in Hungary were largely engaged in fighting the Russian forces, not deporting

---

14. Private letter from my father, in my records.

Hungarian Jewry. That effort largely fell on Hungarian national and local forces.

The Arrow Cross takeover on October 15, 1944, severely worsened the situation of Budapest Jewry. With the countryside "clean" of Jews, the Arrow Cross turned its focus on Jews living in the nation's capital. Accounts paint a horrific picture. The violence was unremitting, and oftentimes undisciplined and devoid of command structure and purpose. Arrow Cross soldiers who killed Jews were at odds with their superiors and with Hungarian policemen.

That, however, did not provide sustenance to the city's beleaguered and vulnerable Jews. The effort to destroy Budapest Jewry failed because the Soviet Army liberated Budapest.[15] Otherwise, the fate of Budapest Jewry would be akin to Jews of the Hungarian countryside.

What ultimately saved Budapest Jewry was the element of time. In other words, what differentiated between the two categories of Jews—those living in Budapest from those living in the countryside—was the arrival of Soviet forces. That is, more than any other factor, what prevented the destruction of Hungarian Jewry in its entirety.

The competing forces—the Hungarian Army, the Arrow Cross, the Soviet Army, and the German military—had distinct interests, goals, and capabilities. The plethora of militaries undoubtedly complicates the setting; the lack of clarity regarding the roles of leading individuals has been much discussed and analyzed.

What is of importance to us is whether the Hungarian civilian—the bystander—was complicit in the cruel fate of fellow civilians. In conversations with experts, one is left with uncertainty regarding rescuers, savers, and active resistance in Budapest. There is, however, no uncertainty regarding the countryside: Jews, including my grandparents, were, in the main, not offered assistance. Neighbors did not provide solace or haven. The historical record is clear and damning.

My mother's experiences are painful to read and sobering to ponder while standing in the courtyard; my father's experience in the Bor Labor Camp, liberation by Tito's partisans, and then walking to Bulgaria in the Carpathian mountains without map or compass are, equally, painful and sobering.

---

15. The post–World War II consequences of liberation-occupation are beyond this book's purview.

Neither was aided by a Hungarian: The heroic Swedish diplomat Raul Wallenberg issued my mother and grandmother a "pass"; Tito liberated my father. While the efforts of individual rescuers in Budapest must not go unnoticed, the question of the Hungarian bystander raises profoundly disturbing questions.

I am not interested in collective or national guilt; that is beyond the scope of this project. Rather, I am focused exclusively on the individual who had the chance to provide assistance and made the decision not to do so. The decision not to help is a decision in the same way that offering assistance is a decision. Both reflect conscious decision making.

That decision making, an individual not intervening on behalf of a clearly identifiable victim, is the essence of the bystander. The "crashing down" my father referenced was significantly facilitated by the overwhelming cooperation of Hungarian infrastructure, government and civilians alike.

The first two are unrelated to this project; the third is very relevant to the proposal recommending liability for the crime of complicity as evidenced by nonintervention.

—10—

Moving Forward: The Bystander as Crime

Introduction

The three weeks I spent in Holland, Germany, and Hungary compellingly reinforced the bystanders' importance to the perpetrator. The interviews, meetings, research, and "on-site" visits were essential to my understanding the murder of 6 million Jews required significant bystander complicity. That is unrelated to the active collaboration-participation of officials and citizens alike who were perpetrators, not bystanders.

Victim testimony is both telling and damning:

I arrived at about 6 in the morning; curious people had gathered in front of the building and were gloating over the misery that had befallen their fellow citizens, the Jews. . . . I wound my way through the hateful crowd of people into the building where the unlucky ones were.

From another testimony we learn:

[H]ouse owners and storekeepers stepped in front of their doors and observed at great length the loading of the Jews into the furniture vans. . . . The people living around the Putlitzstrasse station observed in masses from the bridge across how the rails how these transports . . . departed from an open platform . . . and supposedly they knew nothing of these things.[1]

Incorporating the Holocaust had two purposes—one to bring to light my parents' experiences (Hungary), and two, with an eye to addressing the bystander in contemporary society. That is not to say events of today are equivalent to the Holocaust. They do, however, reinforce that the vulnerable victim, whether in Holland in 1943 or on a train in Chicago in 2016, depends on bystander intervention in the face of a violent perpetrator.

This is not a moral equivalency argument. The Holocaust is not the same as an isolated attack on a young woman at Stanford University. However, what is of concern to me is the vulnerability of the lone individual. That can be mitigated were the bystander to intervene. Unlike those who advocate the "do the right thing" argument, intervention must be a legal obligation. That is the most effective manner whereby the victim will be assisted by the bystander.

The only point of inquiry is whether the individual who chooses not to act on behalf of another individual has committed a crime.

The reasons for a negative response are understandable: The state cannot regulate conduct that more comfortably falls into a rubric of morality; crimes of omission[2] should be a limited category; requiring intervention invites danger to the bystander; the social contract is between the individual and the state, not individual and individual; it is not for the state to impose a duty to act when a preexisting relationship does not exist; and strangers cannot be forced to help strangers.

---

1. Marion A. Kaplan, *Between Dignity and Despair*, Oxford University Press, Oxford, 1998, p. 198.
2. Lionel H. Frankel, Criminal omissions: A legal microcosm, *Wayne Law Review* 11, 1965, pp. 367–429.

The arguments are compelling. However, they fall short. The best proof of their falling short are Hitler's victims. The consequences of bystander nonintervention are clear.

Circumstances and Physicality

Caution is necessary when proposing bystander complicity be codified as a crime. Overreach is dangerous and counterproductive. Codification must focus on the bystander physically positioned to provide assistance to the victim.

The issue of circumstances and physicality is of great importance. That was very clear in the context of the Amsterdam bicycle accident.[3] That incident clearly illustrates both the scope and limit of the proposed legislation; the two—individually and together—define which bystanders would be required to act and which fall outside its proposed range.

Let us carefully examine two contemporary examples. Both cases are deeply disturbing; they have, justifiably, attracted significant media attention and public commentary. Public attention is due, in part, to the fact both are sexual assaults that occurred on college campuses. Understandably, this is an issue that has garnered significant media coverage, forcing college administrators to directly address student conduct.

Outrage has been expressed regarding particular aspects of both cases. That outrage is shared by this writer.

The perpetrators in both cases have had their crimes adjudicated before a court of law; in both cases, the perpetrator was convicted. However, as reprehensible as the criminal conduct was—and it certainly was—the perpetrators are not the focus.

A summary of the facts reads as follows:

Stanford University

Just after 1 a.m. on January 18, 2015, law enforcement officers responded to a report of an unconscious female in a field near the Kappa Alpha fraternity house, according to a sentencing memo.

---

3. See p. 124.

They found the victim on the ground, in a fetal position, behind a garbage dumpster. She was breathing but unresponsive. Her dress was pulled up to her waist. Her underwear was on the ground; her hair disheveled and covered with pine needles.

> *About 25 yards away, two men, passersby, had pinned down and restrained a young man who was later identified as (Brock) Turner.*
>
> *"We found him on top of the girl!" one of the men said. Turner smelled of alcohol as he was handcuffed.*
>
> *One of the men later told authorities that Turner had been on top of the motionless woman.*
>
> *"Hey, she's f—unconscious!" one of the men yelled. Turner managed to get away briefly but the man tripped and later tackled him. Turner was held down until deputies arrived.*
>
> *A witness told investigators that the day of the assault "he saw a female subject lying on the ground behind the dumpster . . . He also noticed a male subject standing over her with a cell phone. He was holding the cell phone. The cell phone had a bright light pointed in the direction of the female, using either a flashlight app in his phone or its built-in flash."*

According to the probation document, Turner told deputies that he walked away from the frat house with the victim and they kissed.

They ended up on the ground, where he removed the victim's underwear and digitally penetrated her for about five minutes, Turner told deputies. "He denied taking his pants off and said his penis was never exposed."[4]

Vanderbilt University

On June 22, 2013, a woman met up with Brandon Vandenburg at a popular bar near Vanderbilt University. She could not remember a period of hours between sipping a blue drink Vandenburg gave her at the bar and waking up in his bed, alone and in the worst pain she's felt, at 8 a.m. the next day, she said.

---

4. http://edition.cnn.com/2016/06/10/us/stanford-rape-case-court-documents/.

He told her that she had gotten drunk and he had taken care of her, and that she had consented to having sex with him. Three days later the woman discovered the devastating truth.

That was the day the woman went to get a three-hour medical exam known as a rape kit. Detectives convinced her to go after seeing surveillance video of her being carried into Vandenburg's dorm, unconscious.

Vandenburg's cell phone showed Internet searches in that same time period, including "can police recover deleted picture messages." One Officer Gish found the deleted pictures and videos of the rape about a week later.

They showed, according to trial testimony:

Vandenburg carried her unconscious body into his room at Gillette Hall about 2:30 a.m. June 23, 2013, asking three teammates he ran into outside for help. They put her on the floor and at least two of them penetrated her with their fingers and one sat on her face, raising his middle finger for a photograph, according to trial testimony.

Vandenburg could not get an erection, so he watched pornography on his laptop.

He tried to wake up his roommate on the top bunk, saying "we have this b—in here" and "we're gonna f—her."

Vandenburg sent videos to four friends and destroyed condoms.

The man she trusted giggled and goaded his teammate, "squeeze that s—," referring to a bottle in her anus.

The Complicity and Culpability of the Bystander (aka, How to Succeed in Rape Culture Without Trying)

The two perpetrators, Brock Turner (Stanford) and Brandon Vandenburg (Vanderbilt), are beyond the scope of our inquiry.

Similarly, the public discussion regarding the rape, drinking, "hook up," and "macho-masculine" athletic culture[5] at U.S. colleges is left to others.

Our sole focus is assessing the *complicity and culpability* of the bystander.

To do so requires examining in detail the decisions of the three bystanders—two at Stanford, one at Vanderbilt. As previously noted, *both action and nonaction reflect a conscious, knowing decision.*

The question is whether the decision is punishable.

Stanford

Two individuals riding their bicycles noticed at 1 a.m. a man on top of a woman behind a dumpster on a path on the Stanford campus. Their attention was drawn by her seeming unconsciousness.

When they called out to the male, he ran; they gave chase, pinned him down and called law enforcement.

The question before us is whether they would be culpable—in accordance with how I define bystander complicity—for not intervening on her behalf.

Stanford Bystanders

The hour was late, the bystanders were riding bicycles and intimacy on college campuses is a reality. This particular location was not known to be a common "coupling" location.

Vanderbilt

The victim was brought by Vandenburg to his dormitory room when she was unconscious; she was repeatedly raped and sodomized. Vandenburg was unable to engage in sexual intercourse because of his drunken condition; however, he encouraged others to rape the victim, recorded the crime, and shared the video with others.

---

5. Turner is a nationally ranked swimmer; Vandenburg played football.

Vanderbilt Bystander

The bystander, a fellow football player, pretended to be asleep on the upper bunk while the victim was raped, sodomized, and otherwise violated for over thirty minutes, by his roommate and others. The bystander, Mack Prioleau, pretended to be asleep as the rape occurred just a few feet away: He testified that he knew exactly what was going on but failed to intervene because the situation "made him uncomfortable."

Apparently, when faced with the choice to either have an uncomfortable conversation with his roommate, or enable a violent rape, the bystander chose the latter. At some point later in the night, he left the room and went to another room in the dormitory.

After the rape, the bystander again chose not to help the victim; during his testimony, he admitted to helping cover up the crime by texting another member of the football team, telling him to "keep his mouth shut" about the rape. The next day, the bystander mopped the victim's vomit off the floor. At no point did the bystander call the police, call for an ambulance, or check on the victim's well-being.

The bystander was not the rapist—but his choice of inaction demonstrates a vicious passivity, where doing nothing is the preferred path of least resistance. Mr. Prioleau was not charged with any crime, nor was he suspended from the university.

The Vanderbilt bystander manifests the consequences of nonintervention and demonstrates why it is appropriate and just to impose criminal liability. There is no doubt Mr. Prioleau had every opportunity to act on behalf of the victim; nevertheless, he made the conscious decision not to do so.

The choice not to act was an unequivocal decision Mr. Prioleau made; in deliberately choosing nonaction, he consciously facilitated the perpetrators' conduct and deliberately placed the victim in greater danger.

The fact Tennessee authorities chose not to prosecute him reflects the failure of the legislature to protect victims. What, after all, is at the core of bystander complicity legislation if not an additional, and much needed, mechanism whereby *victims* can be protected.

Based on the bicycle accident,[6] I would suggest the following:

1. Had the two bicyclists not intervened, they would not be liable for the crime of nonintervention. Given the late hour it was difficult to see, they were riding their bicycles which affects ability to perceive events, and the activity the victim and assailant were engaged in was not "out of place" on a college campus, though the specific location was not considered common for "hook ups."
2. The roommate is the "poster child" for the legislation I am recommending: He was well aware what the perpetrators were doing to the victim, he was well aware of her physical condition, he was fully awake and fully capable of either expressing strong disapproval regarding the rape or alerting the authorities in any number of different ways. He chose to do nothing. For the consequences and harm to the victim, in this particular case, the bystander must bear liability.

A Duty to Aid a Victim or Report a Crime

California and Tennessee, the states where these crimes took place, both lack duty-to-assist laws that might have proved critical in both deterring the vicious passivity represented by the Vanderbilt bystander, and encouraging and protecting the behavior of the bystanders at Stanford.

That additional protection would be the requirement imposed on bystanders to intervene.

Few states currently have duty-to-intervene statutes. Two states that do, Minnesota and Wisconsin, illuminate the positive role the legislature can and must play in addressing bystander complicity.

Subdivision 1 of *Minnesota Statute* 604A.01, reads as follows:

Duty to assist.

A person at the scene of an emergency who knows that another person is exposed to or has suffered grave physical harm shall, to the extent

---

6. See the diagram on p. 125.

that the person can do so without danger or peril to self or others, give reasonable assistance to the exposed person. Reasonable assistance may include obtaining or attempting to obtain aid from law enforcement or medical personnel. A person who violates this subdivision is guilty of a petty misdemeanor.

Wisconsin Statute 940.34, *Duty to aid victim or report crime*, includes the following provision:

(1)(a) Whoever violates sub. (2)(a) is guilty of a Class C misdemeanor.
   (2)(a) Any person who knows that a crime is being committed and that a victim is exposed to bodily harm shall summon law enforcement officers or other assistance or shall provide assistance to the victim.

As in the Minnesota statute, there is also a provision in the Wisconsin statue that imposes a duty on the rescuer only if their actions may be done in safety and without potential threat to oneself:

(d) A person need not comply with this subsection if any of the following apply:

1. *Compliance would place him or her in danger.*
2. *Compliance would interfere with duties the person owes to others.*
3. *In the circumstances described under par. (a), assistance is being summoned or provided by others.*

Had California or Tennessee adopted and enforced duty-to-act statutes such as these, the bystander in the Vanderbilt case would have been found guilty of an actual crime. This scenario is not as daunting as it might seemingly be on its face. Currently, every state has mandatory child-abuse reporting laws that help protect children by obligating non-offending adults to file a report if they have "reasonable grounds" to believe that a child is being abused or neglected.

In other words, a person is obligated to report with a protective-service agency if there is a suspicion of abuse. Duty-to-intervene laws demand much the same as child-abuse reporting laws, with an even easier standard to follow—intervening is a legal duty when one *knows* firsthand that a person is being brutally victimized.

A recommended statute would read as follows:

> *Any person at the scene of an emergency who knows that another person is exposed to or has suffered grave physical harm shall, to the extent that the person can do so without danger or peril to self or others, give reasonable assistance to the exposed person. Reasonable assistance may include obtaining or attempting to obtain aid from law enforcement or medical personnel. A person who violates this section shall be fined not more than $500.*[7]

The statute might also impose a criminal record.

However, limits are necessary in drafting such statutes because it would be self-defeating to recommend unfeasible and impractical legislation. For that reason, the Stanford example is particularly relevant: It would be unreasonable to demand—legislatively—that the two bicyclists intervene.

The *physicality of the circumstances*—nighttime, and therefore limited visibility and the "not out of place" conduct of victim and assailant—would free the two bicyclists of criminal liability had they chosen not to act. The fact they did so is to their credit for which they are to be commended.

Unlike Mr. Prioleau, these two bicyclists were not bystanders who would bear criminal liability for not acting.

Why Punish?

It is not enough to recommend legislation addressing bystander complicity. There are two critical questions that demand an answer: Why punish and to what extent punish? After all, the act of imposing criminal liability

---

7. Jay Logan Rogers, Testing the waters for an Arizona duty-to-rescue law, *Arizona Law Review* 56(3), 2014, pp. 897–920.

on an individual carries much significance, regardless of the extent of the punishment.

Rearticulated, for the state to initiate criminal prosecution against a member of society reflects a profound decision with significant ramifications and consequences. The question whether bystander complicity warrants a criminal process is complex.

The reasons "why not" are easier to answer than "why yes." Demanding a stranger intervene on behalf of another stranger may result in harm; it certainly places the intervening individual in harm's way.

Furthermore, imposing liability requires the bystander to assess the situation at hand; there is always the risk of misunderstanding with its attendant negative fall-out. In addition, requiring an individual to act—and punishing for omission—reflects overstepping by government, legislating what is otherwise considered questions of morality. These are all valid criticisms.

Conversely, the consequences of not requiring bystander intervention are readily apparent, whether in the Holocaust or contemporary society. The examples highlighted throughout this book are just that, examples. It would be possible to bring to these pages countless other examples of the vulnerable victim whose situation could have been alleviated had the bystander chosen to act.

However, in instance after instance bystanders decided not to intervene. That is the essence of bystander complicity.

There is no doubt that rationales are easy to articulate; excuses and explanations are readily available. However, standing in the courtyard where my mother was taken to be shot, retracing the walk of Marcelle Devries, carefully analyzing the scene in the Vanderbilt dormitory room, or considering the violence suffered by an innocent train rider in Chicago make it clear that all four victims could have been provided assistance, and haven, had the bystander acted.

The consequences of that failure are clear: The train rider was physically harmed and her attackers unpunished; an unconscious woman was left unprotected on the floor, repeatedly raped and sodomized; a Maastricht woman was murdered in Auschwitz; and my mother was at the hands of fascists intent on eradicating Budapest Jewry.

Traditional punishment theories focus on retribution, deterrence, incapacitation, and rehabilitation. The recommendation to punish the nonintervening bystander is predicated on deterrence; that is, by meting out punishment on a nonintervening bystander the goal is to deter future bystanders from similarly not acting.

Focusing on deterrence has a twofold purpose—deterring others from failing to intervene and simultaneously expanding the social contract. The essence of deterrence is an attempt to ensure others in a similar situation will act differently than the punished individual:

> *The concept of deterrence is quite simple—it is the omission of a criminal act because of the fear of sanctions or punishment. While not the entire premise, deterrence is certainly an important foundation of the criminal justice system. Law enforcement exists both to apprehend wrongdoers and to convince would-be wrongdoers that there is a risk of apprehension and punishment if they commit a crime.*[8]

Allowing the bystander to go unpunished is to—literally—ensure the four examples above will repeat themselves. That is not to suggest a second Holocaust is imminent; it is, however, to remind us that *the Mack Prioleaus are far more common than the two bicyclists.* We celebrate the Stanford bystanders because of their infrequency and uniqueness.

They should be congratulated. However, we must not create an illusion whereby they are the norm. They are not. Mr. Prioleau represents a clear-cut example of bystander nonintervention.

The harms caused to victims are graphically described above. Harms have been one of the dominant themes throughout this book. Those harms have been caused, primarily, by perpetrators whose actions have been facilitated by the bystanders' decision not to intervene.

That decision—conscious, rational, and knowing—must be penalized. Penalty is only possible when society defines an act as a crime. Although the recommended punishment for the crime of nonintervention would be

---

8. http://scholarlycommons.law.northwestern.edu/cgi/viewcontent.cgi?article=7363&context=jclc, Raymond Paternoster, How much do we really know about criminal deterrence, *Journal of Criminal Law and Criminology* 100(3, Summer), p. 766.

a fine, rather than incarceration, the act would impose on the convicted bystander a criminal record.

The theory of deterrence is particularly applicable as punishment would—it is hoped (expected)—result in others, in similar situations, to act very differently from Mr. Prioleau.

> *Research into Mr. Prioleau shines disturbing light on his seeming failure to understand the ramifications of his decision. Social media reflects/suggests a young man unremorseful, unrepentant, and unable to fathom the consequences of bystander non-intervention:*
> *Mack Prioleau hails from Fort Worth, Texas and is currently studying at Vanderbilt University. During his freshman year, Mack was a member of the Vanderbilt Football team. This past semester, Mack spent his semester abroad in Cape Town, South Africa. Cape Town has provided an opportunity to study at a great institution while pursuing his interests outside the classroom. As someone who enjoys spending their time outdoors, Cape Town was the perfect place to travel. Mack Prioleau is an avid outdoorsman, especially when it involves surfing, fishing, hunting or hiking. Mack has traveled extensively over the past several years. Check out Mack Prioleau's videos to learn more about his travels as well as some travel/outdoors tips and advice.*[9]

It is that casualness, almost insouciance, that is particularly disturbing. That is in direct and dramatic contrast to the impact on the victim. That attitude should come as no surprise for that is—in many ways—the essence of the bystander. As Robert Gellately wrote, "without the active collaboration of the general population it would have been impossible for the Gestapo to enforce these kinds of racial policies."[10]

The bystander facilitates the perpetrator. The bystander's nonintervention decision accentuates the victim's vulnerability in the face of imminent harm.

---

9. https://www.youtube.com/user/mackattack124.

10. Robert Gellately, *Backing Hitler: Consent and Coercion in Nazi Germany*, Oxford University Press, Oxford, 2001, p. 135.

That is the case with Mr. Prioleau; that is the case with Holocaust bystanders.

The four individuals referenced above—the Vanderbilt rape victim, the Chicago train victim, Marcelle Devries, and my mother—are evidence of this reality.

—11—

Where Do We Go From Here?

Where do we go from here? What have we learned from the Holocaust that can be applied to contemporary society?

For me, this book has been a personal journey though that was not its original intention. What started out as a book examining a particular legal question became, over the course of time, something very different. During the course of my research, particularly when it transitioned from the abstract to the personal, the objective legal analysis took on a different tone.

There were many difficult moments, none more so than standing in the courtyard where my mother was to be shot and the day spent in my father's hometown. Speaking with others who have undertaken similar "Holocaust roots trips" reinforces their pain and poignancy.

I do not think my visit differs from those of my friends who have traveled alone, in groups, or with parents to see where the Nazis and their collaborators made the deliberate decision to destroy European Jewry. Although the Final Solution, as decided upon on January 20, 1942, in a beautiful villa in Wannsee, was not fully implemented, that is not for a lack of remarkable and determined effort. After all, when Eichmann's deputy asked my father—on March 19, 1944—"what are you doing here," the war effort as traditionally understood was all but lost. The decision to invade Hungary and in fifty-six days deport 450,000 Hungarian Jews reflects the overwhelming obsession the Nazis and their Hungarian collaborators had with murdering Jews. Although nuances are a matter of dispute among historians, the bare-boned facts cannot be ignored: 6 million Jews were brutally murdered, my paternal grandparents among them.

When M asked me, "how did this happen," I did not imagine coming face to face—very painfully—with the last days of my grandparents' lives. Retracing their walk, house to train platform, will be indelibly stamped into my memory till my dying breath. I did not realize how powerfully the experience impacted me until returning to my Budapest hotel room. I felt that I had come as close as possible to touching two people whom I had never met.

And why is it that they were denied the opportunity to engage with their only grandchild? There are a number of reasons—the three most obvious are those that sealed their fate in Wannsee, those that forced them to board the train to Auschwitz, and those that watched them walk to the damned platform.

The first category either committed suicide or were prosecuted, in some cases, executed. The second category in far too many cases were able to meld back into society after the war, and in other cases were prosecuted where their periods of incarceration, if convicted, were short and oftentimes commuted. The third category is the subject of this book. They were, without doubt, complicit bystanders.

While prosecuting them is neither feasible nor possible in 2016, that cannot be said for today's bystanders. Historical lessons and analogies are complicated, complex, and fraught with risks. That, however, is not a reason not to apply lessons learned. The caveat: A thoroughly symmetrical coupling between events in 1944 and 2016 is intellectually dishonest.

In focusing on the individual, and the decisions individuals make, my focus is specific. Did "person A" intervene on behalf of "person B"? That is my sole point of inquiry.

Because I am neither a moralist nor an ethicist, my inquiry is limited to the law. I have, in the preceding pages, sought to convince the reader that the law must come to the assistance of the vulnerable victim.

Creating a mechanism whereby a bystander, positioned and capable to intervene, is obligated to act is the most profound lesson I have learned since undertaking this project. That obligation, for it to be effective and enforceable, must be rooted in the law. That requires legislature initiative. Thereafter, law enforcement and prosecutors must aggressively act to bring bystanders to court. It is hoped that the nation's judiciary will understand the seriousness of the matter when standing before it is the bystander-defendant.

This undertaking will only be successful if all involved parties recognize how bystander complicity facilitates perpetrator violence. In addition, this requires understanding that the historic reliance on morality is nothing more than a misbegotten illusion. Yes, there always will be bicyclists; the tree-lined rows at Yad Vashem honoring Righteous Gentiles are proof of individuals who acted in a manner befitting their status.

However, those individuals must not mask the reality: Mack Prioleau represents the majority of bystanders. He is the standard, as unfortunate and disturbing as it is. Mr. Prioleau is, on a personal level, of no interest to me. I am repulsed by his callousness.

A football player feigned sleep because the rape made him uncomfortable. His utter disregard for any sense of obligation to act on behalf of a vulnerable victim is, literally, stunning. It merits what can only be a loud, very loud: *Are you kidding me?*

I am deeply sorry he was not prosecuted. He benefited from a terrible gap in the law. That was his good fortune. I can but hope the next Mack Prioleau will feel the full weight of the law.

Which brings me full circle: It is too late to bring the full weight of the law to those who stood by during the Holocaust. Nature has run its course and those individuals have passed. That, however, does not mean that we cannot learn from their behavior and ask how we seek to ensure future bystanders are punished for their complicity should they choose to act in a similar manner.

When standing in front of the Holocaust memorial in Nyíregyháza that includes the inscribed names of my murdered grandparents, I had many thoughts. There was a sense of enormous loss and sadness. There was also a positive: I would like to believe my grandparents would feel pride that their only grandson was standing on blood-filled Hungarian soil honoring their memory. In other words, while they, and millions of others, were killed, the Nazi regime ultimately failed.

However, bystander complicity significantly facilitated perpetrator violence. That applies in the Holocaust and at Vanderbilt. That is not intended to compare the two; it is, however, intended to highlight the impact of bystander nonintervention.

It is for that reason that I am convinced of the requirement to legislate the crime of bystander complicity.

When I said the Mourners' Kaddish at the memorial, it was clear to me that the best way to honor their memory was to make a concerted, determined, and dedicated effort to bring present and future bystanders to justice.

Their complicity must not go unpunished; the complicity of previous bystanders is painful proof of the consequences of nonintervention. No vulnerable victim should pay the price resulting from the decisions of Mack Prioleau.

The price paid by my grandparents is testament to that terrible fact.

Enough is enough.

Criminalizing bystander complicity is a critical step in that essential direction.

Afterword

This book took many turns over the course of four years. What started with M's question—to which I had no answer—has taken me to places I never expected to visit, literally and figuratively. When I decided the issues we were discussing in our runs were book-worthy, my initial thought was to write a traditional "law" book.

Over the course of time, the book took on a more personal tone. The end result is a combination of the two.

Writing about the "law" suggests impersonal, professional writing; writing about one's parents and grandparents is something very different. The first I do regularly; the second I have never done before. The more I researched, the deeper I got into the subject matter, the clearer it became to me that writing this book presented me with a unique opportunity to bring their experiences to light.

I was somewhat hampered in this effort: I am not a trained historian or genealogist. In addition, I am not a natural storyteller nor do I have training or experience in writing personal-family histories. Furthermore, my opportunity to interview family members was very limited: My paternal grandparents murdered in Auschwitz left no record or diary; my father's cognitive skills were greatly impacted, and my mother was very conflicted regarding the project.

The decision to transition from a purely law book to a "combination" project had its complications. Although it was important for me to share their story with the reader, I wanted to do so respectfully and accurately. I did not want to engage in sentimentality or take liberties with facts and circumstances. I was not writing a book that could be defined as "based on historical events."

I was hoping to better understand the bystander through their experiences. That required focusing on the bystander, the victim, and the relationship between the two. I knew very little about literature regarding the bystander; my knowledge was largely limited to what I had heard about Kitty Genovese. That changed when I read Dr. Victoria Barnett's outstanding book, *Bystanders: Conscience and Complicity during the Holocaust.*[1]

At M's urging (and help) I reached out to Dr. Barnett; she graciously invited me to visit her at the U.S. Holocaust Memorial Museum in Washington, D.C. That visit was critical on a number of different levels: Dr. Barnett and her colleagues found a speech my father had previously delivered in Budapest, which they graciously translated into English. That speech served as the core of a small book my mother and I self-published in honor of my father's ninetieth birthday.

In addition, the staff at USHMM was able to provide me with documents regarding my father's journey from Budapest to Bor and subsequently to Palestine. I had never seen these, much less knew of them. The reason for that was simple: My father had never really shared his Holocaust experiences with me. That was absolutely true regarding my mother. The more material I received from the USHMM the more I began to feel like a detective piecing together a story of a world that no longer exists.

However, because I was writing a book that went beyond the personal, I had to learn about the Holocaust, Europe, and World War II. Although I had been a history major in college, my knowledge regarding the history of the events of 1933–1945 was very limited. I undertook what can only be called a one-person course; I read as much as possible. The more I read, the more I realized how little I knew; the more I realized how little I knew, the more I read.

As M repeatedly reminded me, the reading, as interesting as it was, must have a focus and purpose. After all, as she stated on a number of occasions, I am not writing a new history of World War II or of the Holocaust.

Rather, the reading must enable me to answer the question whether the bystander is complicit in harm to the vulnerable victim. In other words, the readings—broad as they may be—must serve a specific purpose. That

---

1. Greenwood Press, Santa Barbara, CA, 1999.

advice was instrumental regarding *how* I read the works of historians and other scholars.

A conversation with my college roommate and great friend, the Rev. John C. Lentz, Jr., on the deck of his home in Cleveland Heights, Ohio, with cigars in hand, was essential to the narrowing of my focus. Lentz[2] and I discussed the role of the church in the Holocaust. We did so from two distinct perspectives—the conduct of Pope Pius XII and sermons given by German pastors during the Nazi period. Regarding the first, there is extensive literature; regarding the second, we were not sure. My take-away from that conversation was that the question of institutional complicity, whether the Catholic Church or Lutheran pastors, was beyond my scope of interest. That conversation crystalized the book's focus—the individual, not institutional, bystander.

That decision was critical for it enabled me to develop a more cohesive approach.

One of the important questions was how to address contemporary bystander dilemmas: Although I intended to examine Europe's current refugee crisis, I ultimately decided not to do so.

Rather, with thanks to Christine Hashimoto, who began working on the book as a research assistant and continued working on it as an attorney, I decided to examine the contemporary bystander through the lens of sexual assaults on college campuses.

Disturbingly, the cases are endless; the number of passive bystanders inexplicable and unforgiveable. The Vanderbilt rape case discussed in Chapter 11 is but one of many. The list is long and should be a source of never-ending shame to bystander and institution alike.

The reprehensible conduct of Baylor University,[3] its former Chancellor Kenneth Starr,[4] and former football coach Art Briles[5] should serve as very clear and loud warning signs to all. I did not discuss Baylor University, and its sanctimonious, hypocritical, and shameful behavior, because

---

2. Lentz's college honors thesis was on Dietrich Bonhoeffer, an interest he shares with Dr. Barnett.

3. https://www.baylor.edu/rtsv/doc.php/266596.pdf.

4. http://www.nytimes.com/2016/06/27/opinion/ken-starrs-squalid-second-act.html?_r=0.

5. http://www.usatoday.com/story/sports/ncaaf/2016/05/26/baylor-fires-art-briles-football-sexual-assault/84973662/.

my focus is on the individual bystander. Nevertheless, its importance in the larger context of institutional and individual accountability is critical.

I mention Baylor and my significant conversation with Lentz because both were critical to the book's development: Rather than focusing on institutions as bystander, I deliberately narrowed my scope of inquiry, and doing so enabled me to actually begin writing the book.

The writing, like any other writing project, had its ebbs and flows, its inevitable ups and downs. The downs resulted in additional research, not all of it "on point"; on more than one occasion, Lentz and M implored me to stop reading and start writing.

They were, of course, correct.

The writing was significantly enhanced by meetings with a wide range of people in different countries. The research, then, went far beyond reading the works of others. It became clear, once I decided that the book would incorporate personal stories, that I needed to spend significant time traveling. In addition to Israel (where my family resides), I traveled to Holland, Germany, and Hungary. However, traveling to these three countries was but the first step in gathering information.

The key question was whether I would meet with Holocaust survivors, bystanders, and others who had firsthand experience. I felt that conversations with scholars, while undoubtedly important, were insufficient for my purposes. To truly understand the bystander-victim relationship required hearing from those who were there. There was, frankly, a sense of a race against time. The number of those alive at the time is dwindling daily.

I knew two things: The meetings would be difficult, and I needed help to organize these meetings.

I was beyond fortunate.

I can count on one hand the number of people who chose not to meet with me. That was their decision and obviously I respected that. There is nothing easy in opening your door to a stranger.

The stories people shared with me were emotional; for some, it was the first time they had spoken about certain aspects of the Holocaust. I was struck by how people came to the meetings: well dressed, highly prepared, and willing to share. It goes without saying I am deeply in their debt.

The conversations enabled me to better understand the Holocaust on an individual level; I wanted to retrace, literally and figuratively, the interaction between bystander and victim. I find the perpetrator uninteresting, whether the senior official or the thug beating a helpless Jew. While reading about both was essential to better understand the workings of the Holocaust, my focus was the individual bystander. The person who chooses not to intervene.

To truly understand the bystander required re-creation of the physicality of the one event that, for me, became an obsession—the walk to the train station from home or ghetto. What happened on the platform was critical. It was the perpetrator who forced Jews onto trains; it was the bystander who could have acted to save the Jew during the fateful walk.

I tried to break the walk down into small segments. I chose two in particular: Marcelle Devries' walk from house to school and my grandparents' walk from house to train station. In retracing/re-creating I sought to understand the physicality. I developed mental images of time of day, weather, where people stood, who saw what, who knew what, and who did what.

My conversations increasingly focused on these specific points. There were times I felt like a detective, putting together the pieces of a crime. But, the crime was not "crime against humanity" but rather a crime against specific individuals. In other words, my efforts were to personalize; to deliberately use names of victims.

That was deliberate as I wanted to humanize the bystander-victim relationship: Someone spat at my grandfather, someone saw Marcelle Devries, someone humiliated my father, someone saw my mother about to be shot, someone yelled at my grandmother.

To achieve this required taking the reader back in time. To do that forced me to travel to Holland and Hungary and, literally, "walk the walk." Maastricht was bearable; Budapest and Nyíregyháza were brutal, almost unbearable. As prepared as I was, nothing compares to actually standing in the very locations where my parents and grandparents were subjected to evil.

Standing in these locations was overwhelming. The question was how would I convey this to the reader. It was not enough to gather stories and to visit places. That was important but insufficient. The challenge was to cohesively and coherently present the material I gathered. That is, the detective work was but one piece of the larger puzzle.

I had to decide what voice to adopt—the detached scholar or the angry son-grandson. There was no uniform decision on my part; it is fair to state that in Hungary I felt anger and resentment that never percolated in Holland or Germany. However, as much anger as I felt I can but hope it did not color my analysis of the bystander. That said, while I sought to avoid "*j'accuse*," it was important the reader understand the intimacy of the bystander-victim relationship.

The relationship was visceral, immediate, and physical; it was not abstract, amorphous, or intellectual. To convey that required being direct in my descriptions; pulling punches would be counterproductive and self-defeating. I drew enormous strength from those who agreed to meet with me. They were direct and honest with me; I needed to be direct and honest with the reader.

While writing this book my father passed away. There is no doubt that his death was an important spark; from October 2015 to June 2016 I wrote a great deal. I believe the tone of my writing changed after his death, becoming more personal, less detached.

That is probably a natural reaction. I do not believe he would agree with the emotional aspect of my writing; he was able—more than me— to detach himself from the topic he was addressing. In writing about what led to my grandparents' murder, I did not feel a detached eye was appropriate. That can be left to others.

I wrote this book in a number of locations, sometimes late at night in hotel rooms after finishing interviews; sometimes in my apartment in Salt Lake City, Utah; sometimes in my family's home in Mevasseret, Israel. Some writing moments were very difficult. To that end, music was very helpful.

The following artists carried me through the stresses of writing: Arik Einstein, Yehuda Poliker, Kaveret, Ludwig van Beethoven, the University of Michigan Marching Band, and the amazing Hapoel Jerusalem (basketball) fans. YouTube is amazing!

Obviously, exercising, a daily routine for me, was essential. While I run and work out regularly, an interesting thing happened to me while writing this book: For the first time in decades, I took up swimming—hesitatingly at first but with greater confidence over time. My fear of swimming is obviously a direct result of my cousin's drowning; my willingness to take up swimming is clearly directly related to this book.

A Final Word

This book became an emotional look into my family's past in an effort to understand the *complicity* of the bystander. That required looking into a sad and tragic past; that also meant asking people to open themselves to me and share their stories.

The stories I have gathered over the past years are many; the heartache people have shared with me is visceral; the respect I have for those who overcame the evil of 1933–1945 is immeasurable.

The complicity of the bystander is something that deserves our immediate attention for it cannot go unpunished.

Appendix

The "Final Solution": Estimated Number of Jews Killed

Country	Pre–Final Solution Jewish Population	Jewish Population Killed in Final Solution	Percent Killed (%)
Poland	3,300,000	3,000,000	90
Baltic countries	253,000	228,000	90
Germany/ Austria	240,000	210,000	88
Protectorate	90,000	80,000	89
Slovakia	90,000	75,000	83
Greece	70,000	54,000	77
The Netherlands	140,000	105,000	75
Hungary	650,000	450,000	70
White Russia	375,000	245,000	65
Ukraine*	1,500,000	900,000	60
Belgium	65,000	40,000	60
Yugoslavia	43,000	26,000	60
Romania	600,000	300,000	50
Norway	1,800	900	50

(*Continued*)

Country	Pre–Final Solution Jewish Population	Jewish Population Killed in Final Solution	Percent Killed (%)
France	350,000	90,000	26
Bulgaria	64,000	14,000	22
Italy	40,000	8,000	20
Luxembourg	5,000	1,000	20
Russia*	975,000	107,000	11
Denmark	8,000	—	—
Finland	2,000	—	—
Total	8,861,800	5,933,900	67

* The Germans did not occupy all the territory of this republic.
Source: https://www.jewishvirtuallibrary.org/jsource/Holocaust/killedtable.html.

Index

Page numbers followed by f indicate figures.

Book Club Questions

1. Is it appropriate to "use" the Holocaust for examining events of today? Why or why not?
2. To examine bystander complicity, both during the Holocaust and more recently, the author shares some very personal stories. How do you feel about this approach, and how did it affect your understanding of the issues?
3. Why do you believe the author's father did not share his son's position on complicity and the bystander?
4. How should complicity be defined? How should bystander be defined? Do you agree with the author's definitions?
5. Can we not rely on individuals doing the right thing? Do we need to impose legal obligations on the bystander to act? Is it dangerous?
6. Who reports on the bystander? Is there the possibility that we will become a reporting society? Is that also dangerous?
7. Shouldn't concern for "my family" outweigh my obligation to someone I have never met and to whom I owe no obligation?
8. In the context of sexual assaults on college campuses, why should we impose a "duty to act" on peers?
9. Is there a danger of "false reporting," thereby casting aspersions on others? Why or why not is it worth the risk?
10. What should be the appropriate punishment for the nonintervening bystander? Would the broader public be amenable to imposing a duty to act and potential punishment on the bystander?
11. Should bystander obligation be extended to events not in our immediate environment (Syria, as an example)? If so, how might this be done?

12. Can nations be bystanders or should the focus be on individuals? Why do you believe this?
13. How do we educate regarding the "duty to act," and what is the appropriate age at which to begin this education?
14. How can we use the Holocaust to draw lessons for contemporary society?
15. Is there anything in the book that challenged your beliefs about bystanders and what they could or should have done? What surprised you?